CITIZENSHIP & CHRISTIANITY
Assembly material combining the two

CLARE RICHARDS

kevin
mayhew

First published in 2003 by
KEVIN MAYHEW LTD
Buxhall, Stowmarket, Suffolk, IP14 3BW
E-mail: info@kevinmayhewltd.com

KINGSGATE PUBLISHING INC
1000 Pannell Street, Suite G, Columbia, MO 65201
E-mail: sales@kingsgatepublishing.com

9 8 7 6 5 4 3 2 1 0

ISBN 1 84417 080 2
Catalogue Number 1500594

Cover design by Jonathan Stroulger
Illustrations by Joanne Aston
Edited by Peter Edwards
Typeset by Fiona Connell Finch
Printed in Great Britain

Contents

Each section is divided into:

1. Suggestions from the syllabus

2. Sacred writings: readings and reflections

3. Outstanding examples from history and today

4. Extra material

5. Prayer and hymns (taken from *Our Songs*, Kevin Mayhew, 1998)

6. Suggestions for follow-up work

7. Vocabulary (suggested by the syllabus)

1. Introduction

Based on Unit 1 of Citizenship syllabus

> In our school, citizenship is central to all we do. All our children contribute to decision-making and organisation, taking more responsibility as they get older. Citizenship is more than part of our curriculum, it is a way of life for the whole community.
> (Dame Mavis Grant, Headteacher, Canning School, Newcastle upon Tyne)

This quotation introduces primary school teachers to the **Citizenship** pack produced by the Department for Education and Skills, QCA in 2002, when the teaching of 'Citizenship' became compulsory in our schools.

Two things became immediately apparent to me, a retired teacher with time to spend on reflection. Firstly, I imagine every teacher in the country is wondering how to fit another compulsory subject into the packed timetable. Secondly, as a Religious Education specialist who worked in Catholic schools, I cannot fail to notice that Dame Mavis Grant's Mission Statement for her school is a secular expression of a Mission Statement that describes a Catholic school. Such a statement could be as follows:

> In our school, our religious faith is central to all we do. All our children, parents and staff contribute to building a community based on Gospel values, with our children taking more responsibility as they get older. Our faith is more than part of our curriculum; it is a way of life for the whole community.

A near lifetime of teaching and parenting has taught me that the two statements above are not exclusive of each other. Some words of the South African Archbishop Desmond Tutu will explain what I mean. He said: 'Our God does not permit us to dwell in a kind of spiritual ghetto, cut off from the real life out there. . . . Our Christianity is not something we put on, like our Sunday best, only for Sundays. It is for every day. We are Christians from Monday to Monday.' He lived this out by entering into the political struggles of his people. He demonstrated that Christian people have a duty to build up their local and national community in a conscientious way. This means that citizenship of the earthly kingdom is important to those who believe they are also living in the Kingdom of God.

With this in mind I have written this assembly book. My aim is to offer our over-busy teachers a way of combining their Citizenship teaching with their religious teaching. It is always helpful to have some readings, stories and prayers, put together under one binding, as assembly material. The chapters are based very closely on the Citizenship syllabus.

I hope that this book will be a useful, time-saving aid for teachers as they persevere, day by day, to inspire their children to become responsible and good citizens of God's world.

A Note for Teachers

Dear Teachers, far be it from me to suggest to you how to prepare an assembly! You are renowned for the creativity, music and colour you are able to bring to these community gatherings. This book is not intended to compete with your experience and skill. As a recently retired teacher, it occurred to me that the new prescription to include Citizenship in the timetable added just one more headache for you: 'How do we fit it in?'

I have more time than you have, and thought it would be helpful if I gathered together readings, stories, poems and songs on all the topics you have to address in the Citizenship syllabus. In this way you can dip into the book for ideas. As an RE specialist I can see many relationships between Religious Education and Education in Citizenship. Assemblies seem a good place to show that we are citizens of both earth and heaven – with heaven beginning on earth.

I have sometimes presumed, in the Introduction to each section, to write as though I were addressing the pupils. It seemed easier to do so. But you are the practitioners, and you will use and adapt the ideas if they are suitable for your classes, and in your own way. I hope the book will be a useful resource, which you can transform into living, lively, worthwhile assemblies.

There is, of course, no reason why you should not use the material in the classroom. You would have a better opportunity, in that setting, to discuss the issues with your pupils.

CLARE RICHARDS

2. Choices
Unit 2 of Citizenship syllabus

1. Suggestions from the syllabus

(a) Right and wrong
(b) Influences on our decision-making
(c) Friends – influence on each other
(d) Rights and responsibilities when
   making decisions

Introduction:

(a) Begin the assembly with a bag of crisps in your hand and start eating them. Comment that you picked the bag up on your way into the hall. It fell out of a pupil's bag; he was walking in front of you. Pause – and ask the pupils if that was a right or wrong thing to do. Why was it wrong?

Ask for examples of wrong things children do in your school. Fights in the playground. Making fun of people. Why is this wrong?

Is it wrong to run down the corridor? Is it wrong because it is a school rule? Why is it a rule? When would it be right to run down the corridor? (To report a serious accident, perhaps.)

(b) Start the assembly by telling the pupils that you have a dilemma. That means you don't really know what to do. Your family have always wanted to visit a new theme park. Your son has come home and said that his friend's family have extra tickets to go next Saturday and have invited you all. Could you perhaps take their grandma in your car as you have more room? Now, your family are excited about the offer and presume you will agree. But you have been looking forward to the local football match, as it is not often you get such a good draw in the FA Cup.

What are you going to do? You have already bought your football ticket and have got an extra one for your son as a surprise. But the rest of your family really want to go to the theme park. And you need the car to get to the match anyway. Why might you decide to go to the match? Why might you decide to go to the theme park?

(c) Start the assembly with a short role-play that you have prepared with three children. The theme is temptation. One girl has not done her homework and she asks a friend to let her copy hers. The third girl tries to persuade the friend to own up to the teacher and accept that she may miss her dinner break. The pupils then discuss the scene with you, and share ideas of their friends being good influences on them.

(d) Start the assembly with two teachers on the platform; one holds a placard saying 'My Rights'. He speaks out: 'It's my right to have a break at dinner time.' The other teacher comes forward with a placard saying 'Your Responsibilities'. She speaks up: 'Yes, but it is also your responsibility to see that your class is looked after at dinner time.' Repeat this with other examples . . .

2. Sacred writings: readings and reflections

We know that some things are right to do and some things are wrong. We probably learnt about this first of all from our parents. If you have a very small brother or sister, listen to your mother or father saying: 'Now don't hit your brother, you will hurt him'; or 'You are a good girl to share your sweets with your sister'.

Why are we taught to choose the good things to do and not the bad things? We do the good things to show that we love and care for other people. The bad things hurt other people. That is why when people live together in a group they make a set of rules that all the group must keep. In that way the people don't hurt each other and can be happy living together. All the people who live in England have to obey the rules of the land. All the teachers and children in this school have to obey the school rules.

Your family probably have a set of rules – What time you must go to bed. How much television you may watch. What time you do your homework – What other rules do you have?

Many people believe that we learn most about right and wrong from our religion. Many religions share the same, or similar, rules. Jews and Christians have the same ten rules, called the Ten Commandments. This is because Jesus was a Jew.

(a) The Ten Commandments (or This is how to live happily)

1. Put God first, before anyone or anything else.
2. Realise that God is greater than any idea you have of him.
3. Use the word 'God' sparingly.
4. Remind yourself that God is with you every day.
5. Love your neighbours by respecting your parents.
6. Love your neighbours by never doing them any harm.
7. Love your neighbours by being faithful.
8. Love your neighbours by respecting their things.
9. Love your neighbours by telling the truth.
10. Love your neighbours by wishing them well.

(From Exodus 20:1-17, retold by H. J. Richards)

(b) Jesus and the greatest Commandment

When someone asked Jesus which was the most important of the Commandments, this is the answer he gave:

> Love God with all your heart,
> And love your neighbour as carefully as you love yourself.
> The whole Bible is based on this. *(From Matthew 22:36-40)*

(c) A Native American Ten Commandments

The North American Chippewa also had Ten Commandments:

1. Never steal, except from an enemy.
2. Respect the aged and listen to them.
3. Be kind to the sick and disabled.
4. Obey your parents.
5. Be modest.
6. Be charitable.
7. Have courage and suffer in silence.
8. Avenge personal and family wrongs.
9. Welcome people to your home.
10. Pray to the Great Spirit.

Jesus would have disagreed with two of these commandments. Which ones?

(d) A very important Jewish Commandment

The Jews believe God gave them 613 laws including the Ten Commandments. They are written down in the first five books of the Bible, called the Torah. They also have a commentary about these laws and other laws worked out and written down much later in a book called the Talmud. The Torah states the law, and the Talmud gives details of how it must be carried out. Here is an example:

The first Commandment is: 'Put God first, before anyone or anything else.' The Jews take this very seriously and keep one day of the week as a special day to be kept 'holy'. It is called the Sabbath day (and is kept on Saturday).

> Remember the Sabbath day and keep it holy. You shall do all your work on six days, but the seventh day is the day God rested from his work of creation: you shall not do any work . . . *(Exodus 20:8-10)*

This is the Sabbath law, written down in the book of Exodus, one of the Torah books. The Talmud gives more detail about work. There are 39 types of work that are not allowed on the Sabbath. For example, Jews may not cook, nor use any type of transport. Jesus himself got into trouble with the authorities because he broke the Sabbath law when he healed a man with a bad arm. Jesus had decided that some laws can be too strict. They may have to be broken occasionally, when someone is in great need. Many Jews would have agreed with Jesus.

(e) Muslim law

Millions of people follow the religion of Islam. They are called Muslims. They follow the teachings of Muhammad, who they believe is the last of the great prophets. They call him The Prophet. Muhammad believed that Allah (God) spoke to him, through the Angel Gabriel. The words that he heard were written down in the Qur'an, the holy book of the Muslims. Many of Muhammad's actions and sayings were also written down. These and the Qur'an make up the written law of Islam. It is called *Shariah*.

Shariah law is very strict. Muslims believe that Allah's law must be obeyed, because that is the only way goodness and peace will come to everyone. There are some severe punishments for breaking the law, but forgiveness is also an important part of Islam. Muslims believe that Allah will always forgive those who are very sorry for their sins. This is what Christians believe too.

(f) Friends

Jesus had good friends. He chose 12 special friends to help him in his work of preaching about the Kingdom of God. The Kingdom of God was a way of saying that people would live in God's love, and be loving to everyone around them. Jesus asked his special friends – we call them the apostles – to continue his work after he had returned to his Father in heaven. He chose Peter to be the leader of the apostles.

Sometimes friends can let us down. Sadly, this happened to one of Jesus' special friends. Judas Iscariot became very worried when things became difficult for Jesus. Judas was anxious about his own future, so he changed sides to protect himself. He went to the authorities who were trying to stop Jesus preaching about God's Kingdom and got paid for turning Jesus in to them.

These are the twelve apostles: Peter, Andrew, James the Greater, John, Philip, Bartholomew, Matthew, Thomas, James the Lesser, Simon the Zealot, Jude Thaddeus, and Judas Iscariot.

3. Outstanding examples from history and today

(a) St Thomas More: a martyr who had to make a choice

Thomas More had just about everything going for him. He had a brilliant career as a lawyer in London. He was an important Member of Parliament and Lord Chancellor of England. He was a writer with an international reputation, and a friend of the king, Henry VIII. He was very happily married, with three daughters. When his wife died, he married again and his new wife, Alice, became a good mother to his children.

The family had a lovely home and lived very comfortably. They often entertained important guests and had many happy parties. Everyone liked

Thomas because he was honest and interesting. And he liked to make people laugh. But he could be serious too, and he was especially serious about his belief in God and his Catholic faith.

Everything about his life seemed perfect until the king had an argument with the Pope. King Henry wanted a divorce to end his marriage, and when the Pope refused this, Henry broke off relations with the Catholic Church. Thomas More had a very difficult choice to make. He was in a dilemma. He was friends with the king, but he was loyal to the Pope. The great lawyer put his faith first. He resigned from Parliament and refused to support the king. He was sent to prison in the Tower of London and was beheaded on Tower Hill. He is a saint and martyr because he put God first, knowing that the consequence of this meant his death. He joked with his executioner, telling the crowd, 'I am the king's good servant, but God's first.'

(b) St Maximilian Kolbe: he chose to give his life for another

There was a young boy, called Raymond, who lived about a hundred years ago in Poland. His parents were quite poor but they sent their son to a good Catholic school because they were very serious about their faith. They wanted their children to love Jesus and Mary before anything else. They were a great influence on Raymond. He decided he wanted to be a martyr and die for his strong faith in God.

Raymond was good at his school work, top of the class in science and maths. He became enthusiastic about joining the army, and seemed to like the idea of fighting for his country. But instead he chose to become a Franciscan priest. He would fight for goodness by writing about Jesus and Mary. He changed his name to Maximilian, to show that he was starting a new life.

He was a very successful priest and publisher of Catholic papers. Hundreds of young men joined him until he had to build a monastery to hold 762 new priests. Maximilian wanted to be a missionary so he could spread the Good News about God outside Poland. He went to Japan and became just as popular there. But he fell ill and had to return home. It was a bad time for the Polish people as war was approaching. Germany invaded Poland and Catholic newspapers were banned.

Fr Maximilian had a dilemma. He was advised to close down the press. Pressure was put on him to stop publishing his papers. He refused and was arrested. He was sent to the dreaded Auschwitz concentration camp. He was treated very badly by the guards, but he spoke of God's love to the prisoners and shared his food with them. Finally, Maximilian made a choice that surprised everyone. He volunteered to take the place of a married man who was being sent to the punishment block. He died there and so became the martyr he had always wanted to be.

(c) Gordon Wilson: he chose to forgive

It is a very sad fact that there are often outbreaks of trouble in Northern Ireland. The Catholics don't get on with the Protestants. (It is a problem that goes back many years, mainly about who owns the land.) In 1987 a shocking thing happened in the town of Enniskillen. A bomb exploded in the town centre during a Remembrance Day service at the war memorial. It killed eleven people, including a young nurse, called Marie. Her father, Gordon Wilson, was badly injured.

The BBC cameras went to the hospital and a reporter spoke to some of the survivors. Mr Wilson amazed the reporter, not to mention the world that watched the report. Instead of speaking angrily about the bombers, he said that he forgave them. He was heartbroken that his daughter had been killed, yet he did not condemn the killers. How did he manage to do that?

He told the reporter that he did not understand how God allows such tragedy, but he accepted it as part of God's bigger plan. He believed that he would meet Marie again in heaven. This deep faith shook the people of Northern Ireland. Gordon had made a choice for good over evil. He had chosen to forgive the unknown people who had shattered his family, instead of bitterness and anger. He became known as the 'Voice of Enniskillen'. He spent the next ten years, until his death, working for peace.

How did he get such strength to do this? Perhaps from the influence of his parents. He was the son of a devout Methodist (Protestant) couple. His father was a draper and his mother a nurse. They taught him to respect both Protestants and Catholics. He could never understand why people chose to hate one another. He learnt from his parents that the Christian Gospel is about loving one another and always being ready to forgive.

Gordon had a happy family because they did not take sides in the conflict in Northern Ireland. Gordon once wrote, 'I am happy to try and be a friend to all and an enemy to none.' The world would be a much happier place if everyone could write that.

(d) Anna Gurney: she chose to help her local community in spite of her disability

Probably very few people have heard of Anna Gurney. They know more about her cousin, Elizabeth Fry (see Unit 9, page 74). But Anna, like many very ordinary, good people, took on the responsibility to help her neighbours. When she died in 1857 about 2000 people went to her funeral at St Martin's Church, Overstrand, in Norfolk.

Anna was born in 1795 at Keswick Hall, a beautiful Gurney house near Norwich. The Gurney family were Quakers, peace-loving Christians. They made money in banking and in the weaving business. The Gurneys had many splendid properties in Norfolk. They were rich, but they chose to share their good fortune with others.

When Anna was a baby she became ill with polio and could never walk. She spent all her life in a wheelchair. As she grew older she realised that she had two options: to sit back and be looked after all her life, or to overcome her disability. She chose the second option. She became very active, and even more energetic than her friends.

Anna loved reading and learning new languages. Her family had a holiday home at Northrepps Hall, near Overstrand. She learnt to swim and always loved the sea. Her best friend was her cousin, Sarah, who lived with Anna's family. The two friends spent many hours helping their neighbours, especially when they were in trouble.

Later they left Keswick Hall and moved together into Northrepps Cottage. They joined the Church of England and taught at Sunday School. They used their money to pay for the village school, to support lifeboats and to buy Bibles for the Missionary Society. Anna will always be remembered for helping shipwrecked sailors. When there was a storm her servant wheeled her down to the beach. For over 20 years she directed the life-saving operation, using a line-firing gun to direct the sailors. She bought all the equipment herself. Anna also paid for shipwrecked sailors to travel home.

No wonder it was the fishermen who carried Anna's coffin at her funeral. And these strong men cried as they said goodbye to their friend.

4. Extra material

(a) A true story about people who chose to love their enemy

Russia and Germany were enemies, fighting each other. The Russians took 20,000 German soldiers prisoner. The prisoners were to be marched through Russia's capital city, Moscow. Crowds, mostly women, gathered to stare and shout at their hated enemy. Many of the women had a husband, son or brother killed by the Germans. The police were worried that the crowd could get out of control.

But a strange thing happened. The people started to jeer as the German prisoners came into view. As they came nearer the angry crowd could see that they were thin, dirty, unshaven and many were hobbling on crutches. Others had blood-stained bandages around their heads. The street suddenly became dead silent.

Then an elderly lady pushed past the police and ran up to the line of prisoners shuffling by. She put a piece of bread into a soldier's pocket. Suddenly from everywhere women ran towards the soldiers and gave them bread and cigarettes.

The German soldiers were no longer the enemy. They were people who needed help. (From a story by Yevtushenko.)

(b) A poem

I am me,
and I can be
the kind of person
that I choose to be.

I can choose to share,
I can choose to keep,
to make others laugh,
to make others weep.
I can choose to smile,
I can choose to frown,
to build others up,
or to do them down.
I can choose to be cruel,
I can choose to be kind,
to follow the rest
or know my own mind.

It's my life
and, win or lose,
it's up to me,
because I can choose. (Anon)

5. Prayer and hymn

(a) Our Father in heaven,
    you created all things
    in the heavens and on the earth.
    And as the crown of all your work,
    you created us, human beings,
    to share with you
    the power of continuing to create
    the world around us.
    We turn to you, our creator,
    to help us in this great task.
    Teach us to choose
    what is right and what is good,
    so that our world can live
    in the peace and happiness
    that your Son, Jesus
    prayed and worked for. Amen.

(b) Our Father in heaven,
    thank you for our friends.
    Help us to understand that
    real friends help us:

to choose what is right,
to think of other people,
to speak with kindness,
and to act with honesty.
Our Father in heaven
thank you for our real friends. Amen.

Appropriate hymns:

  61 Don't build your house on the sandy land
  62 Do what you know is right
  78 Friends, all gather here in a circle
109 He gave me eyes so I could see
154 Jesus had all kinds of friends

6. Suggestions for follow-up work

(a) An activity for the week: Choosing to be cheerful or grumpy!

Draw out a page of a diary, by dividing a page of your RE or homework exercise book into eight rectangles or squares. Date each one for the week. At the end of each day draw a face in the appropriate square – either a smiling or a miserable face. You decide which. It should show how you feel you have been for the most part of that day! In the eighth space (at the end of the week) write a comment about the week.

(b) In small groups make up your list of ten commandments for the school. Write them out, with felt-tip pens, on a large sheet of card and display. Compare them. Which are the ones that appear in every list of ten? Why do you think this is?

7. Vocabulary

Dilemma, conflict, pressure, influence, option, alternative, consequence, choice, responsibility.

3. Animals and us
Unit 3 of Citizenship syllabus

1. Suggestions from the syllabus

(a) Human needs – shelter, water,
    food, clothing, etc.
(b) Animal needs
(c) Our responsibility towards animals:
    (i) in the wild (ii) as pets
(d) Animal welfare organisations

Introduction:

(a) Begin the assembly by telling the children you want them to use their
    imagination.
    First: imagine you don't have a house, or flat, or bungalow to live in.
    When you leave school you go to a sort of shack your family have put
    up on a bit of land shared by hundreds of others. Imagine where you
    would put all the things you have in your bedroom in that shack. How
    would you keep them safe?
    Second: imagine that you have nothing to drink at all, for days and
    days. No taps to turn on, no cartons of milk or orange juice, no cups of
    tea. No water at all. Nothing.
    Third: imagine that you have no food at all. You have to search the
    streets and the fields to see if you can find something, anything to eat – a
    few crumbs, a few leaves of a plant. You have no money to go to the shops.
    Fourth: imagine you are really cold and have no warm clothes at all.
    You just have the clothes you are in today, now. Nothing to change
    into, nothing to keep out the cold or the rain.
    Life would be dreadful, wouldn't it, without shelter, water, food and
    clothing?
    All human beings need these things. Not everybody has them.

(b) Ask the pupils some questions: Have you ever thought that animals need
    things too? Animals have to live in homes. Lions live in dens, don't they?
    What animals live in warrens? And what animals live in setts? Can you
    think of other names of animals' homes? And animals have other needs
    too. They have to drink and they have to eat. They don't really need
    clothes though, as we do. They have their own coats of fur or hide. Some
    of you have pets. Where does your pet live? I have a cat, and she thinks the
    whole house is hers. We made her a little bed to sleep in, but she likes to
    sleep in the best armchair or under the radiator in the bedroom.

(c) Have a general talk about responsibility: What does 'responsibility' mean? It means caring for others. It means being trusted to take charge of others or of things around us that need looking after. One of you might be responsible for the library books on your classroom shelf. You must check them and see they don't go missing. Some of you have been made responsible for putting away the PE apparatus correctly.

Needs and responsibility always go together. For example, if your pet needs food, then you are responsible for providing it.

Discuss our responsibility towards: (i) wildlife, (ii) our pets and (iii) farm animals.

(d) Before the assembly collect information about animal welfare organisations. Most public libraries have leaflets or displays about such organisations (usually the local branches) as the RSPCA, the RSPB, the PDSA, etc. Tell the children about the work of the organisations (or prepare a few children to speak about them). Most towns or cities will have local animal rescue sanctuaries. Perhaps invite someone from one of these to an assembly. For example, near Norwich is Redwings Horse Sanctuary, for horses and donkeys rescued from irresponsible owners. Children can 'adopt' one of them and receive information and photos, as well as visit their donkey or horse. You may want to invite a local vet to come and talk to the pupils about caring for their pets.

2. Sacred writings: readings and reflections

Today people in Britain are far more concerned about the animal world than ever before. Sadly this is not true everywhere. In Dorset there is a large monkey sanctuary where there are dozens of apes and monkeys that have been rescued from cruel treatment in circuses and on beaches across Europe. You may want to discuss, in a class follow-up to the assembly, the rights of animals in regard to zoos and circuses. Should animals be kept locked up? Don't they have rights? Some Christians today are concerned that the creation story in Genesis led to the view that human beings have all the rights, and animals are 'at their disposal'. This was clearly the view in the Middle Ages, when theologians like Thomas Aquinas believed animals had no rights at all. We don't think like that today. We have greater respect for all of God's creatures.

(a) The story of creation

The creation of the world is a mystery. Scientists are always trying to discover exactly how it happened. Christians, like the Jews, believe that God created the world and keeps it in being. The Jews, long ago, wrote a poem about the creation of the world. They didn't know exactly how it was done, but they were full of wonder at how marvellous the world is: the sky, the sun, day and night, trees and plants, birds, fishes and animals, and, best of all, human beings. The poem tells a story about God making the world in six days – so he could have a rest on the seventh day. It is a lovely story. The writer made the sixth day of creation the most important, for on that day God created both the animals and human beings.

> God said, 'From the dry land,
> let all kinds of life appear:
> domestic and wild, large and small.'
> And they did, and God saw that it was good.

> Then God said, 'Let there be human beings
> to reflect my own creativity,
> and to care for fish and birds
> and domestic and wild animals.'

> So God created human beings,
> male and female, to be his reflection,
> and gave them his blessing:
> 'Have many children and fill the world;
> it is all in your hands:
> fish and birds and animals, domestic and wild.' *(Genesis 1:24-28)*

(b) The Aboriginal creation story

There are many different stories about the creation – how the world was made. The Aboriginal people of Australia have a great respect for animals; this is explained in their creation story, which they call the Dreamtime.

Long ago giant humans, kangaroos, emus, snakes, koala bears and other animals sprang out of the sea and sky and moved across the flat, empty continent of Australia. Their journey was known as Dreamtime. They had many adventures when they stopped to make shelters and find food. They sang, and they fought. When the journey was finished they didn't die, but sank back into the earth and their spirits are still there today. The places where they sank into the earth have become the mountains, rocks and secret paths. These are full of special, sacred meaning to the Aborigines.

The giant figures of long ago are called the Dreamtime Ancestors. All Aborigines believe that they each have their own particular ancestor and that they are related to many other ancestors. These ancestors may have been animals like the emu or the koala bear. Aborigines 'know' who their ancestor was, and will never kill that animal. It is sacred to them and this is why the Aborigines have so much respect for all animals, even the poisonous snake.

(c) The story of Noah's ark

One of the most well-known stories from the Bible is the story of Noah's ark.

In the very early days after the creation God began to be sorry he ever made the world. Men and women were behaving so badly that God was deeply hurt. But one man cheered him up. He was called Noah, and he was trying to live in God's way. For his sake, God decided to save his family and some animals, but to drown the rest in a big flood. God told Noah to build a large ship and to take his family and a pair of every animal on board, so that they could start up families again, when the flood was over.

And that's what happened. It rained and rained for 40 days. All the land flooded and everything died, except the people and animals on the ship. Noah knew the waters were going down when he sent a dove out to look for dry land. The bird returned with an olive leaf in her beak. They soon left the ship and started up new lives on the dry land. God was sorry he had to be so fierce and he promised that he would never drown his creation again. He put a rainbow into the sky as a sign of his promise.

This is a legend, that is, a story, not a description of something that actually took place. The writer had a message he wanted us to learn from his story. It is this message that is *true*. The storyteller wanted us to know that God loves his creatures, human beings and animals. God will always care for us and for the animals, and he will always give human beings a second chance when they behave badly.

(d) The donkey

There is a well-known legend about the donkey. A donkey appears in the story of Jesus in the Gospels. But the legend is a story made up much later about this donkey, perhaps because it is such a loveable, hard-working animal.

In many hot countries donkeys are work animals. They carry people on their backs as transport. They carry large baskets on their sides, called panniers, to carry fruit and vegetables to the market. They even carry big stones when roads are being built. Donkeys were important animals in Jesus' time. In the Christmas story Mary and Joseph had to go on a long journey to Bethlehem. It doesn't say so in the story, but we imagine that Mary rode on a donkey. It was probably happy to settle down by the side of the manger in the stable. So the legend says that the donkey was present at Jesus' birth.

The Gospel story of Jesus does mention a donkey later on. A week before his death Jesus arrived in Jerusalem. He didn't walk in, he rode in on a donkey. There was a tradition in the land that a man riding in on a horse was riding in to fight, but a man riding in on a donkey was coming in peace. Jesus was a man of peace and so he chose the donkey. But shortly afterwards Jesus was condemned and put to death on the cross. The legend says that this is why every donkey since then has the mark of a cross on its back. Next time you see a donkey, look for the cross.

(e) Jewish law

The Jewish people looked after their animals well. Among their many laws, written in the Torah, are instructions about this.

> If you come across a neighbour's cow or sheep straying,
> make sure you take it home to him.
> If he is not a near neighbour,
> or you don't know who he is,
> take the animal home with you
> and keep it until he comes looking for it,
> and then give it back to him.
> The same applies to a donkey . . .
> or anything else that has gone astray.
> Don't leave it where you find it,
> as if it was none of your business.
> If you come across a neighbour's cow or donkey
> fallen down by the roadside,
> don't go hurrying on your way.
> Help him put it on its feet again. *(Deuteronomy 22:1-4)*

> When you're using an ox to tread out the corn
> don't put a muzzle over his mouth. *(Deuteronomy 25:4)*

(f) From the Book of Proverbs

> Good people take care of their animals
> but bad people are cruel through and through. *(Proverbs 12:10)*

(g) Muslim views

The Muslims have similar instructions and views about animals.

Muslims tell the story of Muhammad and the ants. Once when Muhammad and his friends were on a journey, they stopped for a rest. One of them lit a fire because it was a cold evening. The Prophet Muhammad noticed an ant hill, and saw some ants hurrying towards the fire. He immediately told the man to put out the fire. He was teaching his friends that Allah forbids any creature, even the smallest, to be harmed.

In the Muslim sacred book, the Qur'an, Muslims are told how they must respect and take responsibility for birds and animals. Muhammad told many stories about the importance of caring for animals, because he believed that they have feelings and that their lives have a part in Allah's plan. Farm animals must never be overworked and farm workers have to cut their nails before milking the cows. Young animals must never be sold when they still need their mothers. Muslims are not allowed to hunt animals as a sport. And they do not approve of animals being used in scientific experiments.

(h) The Hindu elephant god

Many people in the world are Hindus. Hindus believe in a supreme Spirit, called Brahman. There are many gods and goddesses who represent the different aspects of Brahman's character. One of the best-loved gods is called Ganesh. He is the elephant-headed god, the god of wisdom, who protects travellers and solves people's problems. Hindus pray to Ganesh whenever something new happens in the family, like moving to a new school. Most homes have a shrine to this god.

In the traditional stories, Ganesh was an ancient forest god. He used to ride around on his friend, the rat. The Hindu religion began in India, where the elephant is a noble and important animal. Cows are also very important animals in India. The Hindu religion believes that they are sacred and may not be killed.

3. Outstanding examples from history and today

(a) St Francis of Assisi

Francis was a happy, carefree young man. This was not surprising because he had a very happy home, plenty of money, good friends, and a loving mother who would do anything for him. He lived in Assisi, a small hillside town in Italy, over 800 years ago. During his lifetime there was fighting in Italy. Francis joined his local army and as an adventurous knight on horseback, he rode out to attack nearby Perugia. His side lost and he was taken prisoner. It was a year before he arrived back home. And he was ill.

Francis had time to stop and think about life. He took a walk one day and visited a ruined church. He seemed to hear Jesus speak from the cross, saying, 'Francis, rebuild my falling church.' He was so keen to start that he sold some of the cloth from his father's business to buy the bricks. His furious father threw him out of the house.

Francis changed his life completely. He dressed in rough clothes, had no money and no home. Yet he was always happy and laughing. Why was this? Because his friends joined him, and together they walked all over Italy, singing and telling the people about God. They did any work offered them in return for food. Francis loved the countryside, the hills and the animals. He joyfully praised God for his wonderful creation. Everyone seemed to love Francis, even the animals. People said that a fierce wolf once sat down at his feet. He talked to the birds, telling them how much God loved them. That is why in pictures or statues of Francis a bird is often sitting on his shoulder. He is the patron saint of animals.

(b) St Brigid of Ireland

Many, many years ago, in the fifth century AD, a kind and charming girl called Brigid lived in Ireland. Everybody loved her. Her father, who was the pagan chieftain called Dubthach, sometimes got cross with her because she used to give away food to the poor. She even gave away his sword. Her mother was a Christian slave, called Brocessa. It was Brocessa who taught Brigid to share what they had with others.

No one was surprised when Brigid said she wanted to be a nun. Nuns chose to spend their lives praising God and helping in the local church. Nuns in those days lived at home, but Brigid thought it was a good idea for a group of nuns to live together in a community. So she set one up. Very soon there were communities of nuns all across Ireland; the biggest one was at Kildare.

From the many stories that were told about Brigid, we know that she was always happy and energetic, and loved music. Brigid was a very important nun and could have lived quite comfortably. But she didn't. She kept giving things away to the poor, and she loved to work hard on the convent farm. She looked after the sheep, made home-brewed ale, and cared for any animal who came her way. She loved animals and wildlife. It was said that she tamed foxes and wild boar. Wherever she went the farmyard ducks followed her.

Brigid lived a life of ordinary hard work and prayer. We call her a saint because she did this so well, and with love for all God's creation. It is no wonder that everyone in Ireland loves St Brigid.

(c) St Cuthbert of Lindisfarne

If you live in the north of England you probably know all about St Cuthbert. He was born in Scotland in 634. He looked after his father's sheep on the hillside above Leader Water. He became a monk in a monastery at Melrose and then became a travelling monk, riding on his horse for hundreds of miles across southern Scotland. He visited all the Christian communities.

On his journeys he grew to love the whole of creation, mountains, rivers, trees, birds and wildlife. He eventually moved to the monastery on the island of Lindisfarne. He was made prior (leader) of the monks and everyone realised he had a great gift in understanding people. He listened to everyone and was able to share people's joys and sorrows.

In the evenings Prior Cuthbert wandered alone in the fields around the monastery, admiring the beauty of nature and praising God for it. He loved to listen to the cry of seabirds over the cliffs. He became their protector. It would be a good idea if St Cuthbert was made the patron saint of the RSPB (the Royal Society for the Protection of Birds).

(d) Native Americans and their respect for animal life

Many people of different religions, and backgrounds, have a deep respect for animals, and will never treat them badly. Amongst these people are the

Native Americans who lived very close to the animal world. They always treated the wild animals, especially the ones they had to hunt for food, with responsibility. They believed that animals have rights. They never killed an animal for sport, but only in order to survive. They used up every part of the animal before they killed another one. Its flesh was their food; the bones were used for tools and the skin became clothing. The Native Americans 'thanked' the animal for giving up its life for them.

A medicine man, Brave Buffalo of the Sioux people, wrote:

> Let a man decide upon his favourite animal, and then study it. He must learn its innocent ways. Let him learn to understand its sounds and move-ments. The animals want to communicate with man, but Wakantanka (the Great Spirit) does not want them to do so directly. Man has to work hard to get an understanding with the animal.

(e) The people of the rainforest

The people of the South American rainforest believe that the forest animals and trees are powerful spirits. They must be respected. The most powerful animal spirit is the jaguar. It is the largest and most feared animal. The witch doctor, called a 'shaman', is believed to turn into a jaguar so that he can visit the spirit world. To do this he dresses up in a jaguar skin with a necklace of jaguar teeth. Sometimes he growls like the mighty animal. Then, in a trance, he asks the spirit to help his tribe. They may be needing more food, or they may be sick.

(f) The Inuit

The Inuit of the Arctic (the term Eskimo apply to the people as a whole) survive in the cold and ice by hunting animals. They hunt whales, walruses, seals and polar bears. They believe that every animal has a spirit, and a special bond is formed between the hunted animal and the hunter. When the animal is killed hunters dance and sing to thank the animal spirit for its meat and its skin. For these people the natural world is awesome; it is feared and respected.

4. Extra material

(a) A poem from the Psalms

1 Praised be the Lord!
    My God, how great you are! . . .

5 You have planted the earth on foundations
    that are firm and will never be moved . . .

10 You make springs gush out of the rock
    and run down between the mountains

to provide water for all animals,
even the thirsty wild donkey;
and in the trees along the banks
the birds make their nests and sing . . .

14 You make the grass grow for the cattle
and plants that people can use
to get the food that they need
and wine to cheer their heart . . .

15 In the trees that God has planted –
the mighty trees that catch the rain –
the birds can build their nests:
the storks live high in the fir-trees.
Wild goats find a home on the mountains,
and rock badgers hide in the caves . . .

21 At night lions come out roaring
looking for the food God provides.
At dawn they slink away
and creep back into their dens . . .

24 What a variety you have created, O Lord,
and with what care you have ordered it all!
All our earth is your creation . . .

33 I shall sing this song as long as I live
and hope to please God as he pleases me. *(From Psalm 104)*

(b) One of Aesop's fables: The Fox and the Crow

Once upon a time there was a fox who lived in the woods. He was always hungry. He ate and he ate until his jaws ached. He crunched up bones and licked his paws and said, 'I'm hungry.' He moaned and he groaned and he said, 'I'm so hungry.' He went for a walk in the woods and up in the tree he saw a crow. He saw a big, shining black crow. The crow had something in his beak. It smelled good. Fox licked his lips and said, 'Yum, yum, yum, that smells like cheese. I must get that cheese.'

The fox looked up at the crow and cried, 'Can you see me, crow?' The crow looked down at the fox and shook his head. He kept his beak shut and winked his little bright eye, and said nothing. Then fox sat down under the tree. 'Oh, crow,' he said, 'I'm dying to hear your wonderful voice. Sing me a song, crow, with your glossy black feathers, with your shiny purple head and your twinkling eye. Sing me a song.' Crow puffed up his feathers with pride. He opened his beak wide. 'Caw! Caw!' sang the crow. 'Ho, ho!' said the fox as the cheese fell to the ground. 'Thank you for your song.' Sly old fox. (What is the moral of this tale?)

(c) 'The Tyger' by William Blake (for the older children)

Tyger! Tyger! burning bright
In the forests of the night,
What immortal hand or eye
Could frame thy fearful symmetry?

In what distant deeps or skies
Burnt the fire of thine eyes?
On what wings dare he aspire?
What the hand dare seize the fire?   .

And what shoulder, and what art,
Could twist the sinews of thy heart?
And when thy heart began to beat,
What dread hand? and what dread feet?

What the hammer? what the chain?
In what furnace was thy brain?
What the anvil? what dread grasp
Dare its deadly terrors clasp?

When the stars threw down their spears,
And water'd heaven with their tears,
Did he smile his work to see?
Did he who made the Lamb make thee?

Tyger! Tyger! burning bright
In the forests of the night,
What immortal hand or eye
Dare frame thy fearful symmetry?

5. Prayer and hymn

(a) Psalm 104 (see page 24).

(b) God our Father,
it was you who in the beginning
created our world, and all its animals
great and small.
We want today to thank you
for the strength of the lion,
the beauty of the horse,
the gentleness of the sparrow,
the dignity of the cat,
the companionship of the dog,
the strangeness of the giraffe,
the grace of the tiger.

Teach us, Lord, to be responsible
for the whole of your creation,
and to care for all your creatures
great and small. Amen.

Appropriate hymns:

  17 All of the creatures God has made
  44 Caterpillar, caterpillar
  74 Fishes of the ocean
238 Rise and shine
322 Who put the colours in the rainbow?

6. Suggestions for follow-up work

(a) Have a class discussion about endangered species.

It is probably true that people in the West, that's us, have never had a very deep respect for animals. Native Americans, peoples of the rainforest and Australian Aborigines always have. In the West, for many years, people believed that animals existed to be farmed and hunted – for food and sport – in any way they wanted. It is only in the last hundred years that some people have become concerned about this. This may be because we have realised that some of the great animals will die out. They are called the 'endangered species'. Animals, especially large wild animals, are becoming scarce. They now need protection from humans. Among these animals are buffaloes, tigers, rhinos, whales, elephants and pandas.

The panda was chosen as the emblem for the WWF (Worldwide Fund for Nature). The WWF is one organisation that works to protect animal life.

There is a big question to ask:

Does it really matter if a species dies out? Should we save these animals? There are other awkward questions:

Do zoos help to protect endangered species, or do they simply treat them as showpieces?

Should circuses have performing animals or performing people?

(b) Make a creation frieze for the classroom. Invite the children to bring photographs of their pets to put on the frieze.

(c) The children could make leaflets with instructions: How to look after your pets.

7. Vocabulary

Needs, rights, care, rules, responsibilities, pets, wildlife, farm, animals.

4. People who help us
Unit 4 of Citizenship syllabus

1. Suggestions from the syllabus

(a) People who help us in the community, especially the police (also ambulance service, fire service, health professionals, teachers)
(b) Dangers they are willing to face
(c) Police and crime. What is right and wrong? Crime hurts others
(d) Why laws and rules?
(e) When laws conflict with each other

Introduction

(a) Begin the assembly by saying, 'This morning we are going to start our assembly by raising three cheers for our parents. *For our mums and dads, 'hip-hip-hooray'*, etc. Now why have we done that? Because mums and dads are the people who help you most. They look after you; they feed you; they nurse you when you are ill; they teach you; they keep you safe; and sometimes they make rules and see you obey them! They do all this because they love you and care about you.

'There are many other people who help all of us. Today we have . . . visiting us. He/she will tell us about the work they do in our local community.' Conclude, after the police officer, nurse or firefighter has spoken, by mentioning other services, for example, refuse collectors, shopkeepers, lawyers.

(b) Make a large card with 'Police Officer' written on it. A pupil will stand on the platform holding it. Repeat this with 'Firefighter', 'Doctor', 'Paramedic', etc. Tell the pupils that all these people take risks, in order to help us. Discuss the risks they might take. What other jobs are dangerous?

(c) Have some children on the platform. They represent the police. They introduce themselves: for example, 'I'm PC Brown, I'm a traffic policeman.' The others could be a community policewoman on the beat; a policewoman who drives a squad car; a policeman who works in the drug squad. Ask what crimes these police officers have to face.
Why is speeding wrong?
Why is driving after drinking alcohol wrong?
Why is vandalism wrong?
Why is stealing from a shop wrong?
Why is mugging wrong?
Why is it wrong to sell drugs? Other questions?

Discuss what links all these 'wrongs'. They hurt other people. Right actions respect other people. Wrong actions damage others (and yourself).

(d) Why laws and rules? Have a copy of the Highway Code. Read out some of the laws.

Ask why we have these rules of the road. What would happen without them? On a large platform some role play could be introduced with traffic lights and a crossing marked out. Pupils could be vehicles at the lights (i) obeying the signs, (ii) ignoring the signs and having a pile-up!

Rules are part of life. Even your family has to have rules. They set a pattern which makes it possible for you to live together as a small community, without chaos.

(e) Give an example of laws conflicting with each other.

What happens if . . . ?

A large store insists that all the staff work Sunday shifts, but a member of staff believes that Sunday should be a special day for going to church, and will not work.

A law states that children have to attend school, but in a family where the father is working on an oil rig, and the mother is sometimes very ill, the eldest child has to stay away from school to look after the mother and baby.

2. Sacred writings: readings and reflections

Every country has laws to live by. Every religion has laws to live by. In many countries the laws are almost identical to religious laws. For example, English law is based on Roman and common law which have been influenced by Christianity's law. This is because most people in England were Christians when the laws were first written.

Some countries in the Middle East, like Iran and Saudi Arabia, have laws based on Islam. The State of Israel is influenced by Jewish law. A good illustration of this is to look at the day of the week when some shops remain closed in different countries:

England – Sunday. This is the holy day for Christians.

Iran – Friday. This is the holy day for Muslims.

Israel – Saturday. This is the holy day (Sabbath) for Jews.

Jesus was Jewish and he grew up with a great love for his Jewish faith. Jesus was a brilliant teacher who could sum up the whole of Jewish law in a clear saying or story.

It is important to remember that, as a Jew, Jesus would have had a great respect for the law. The law books, the Torah, were so sacred that they were kept in the most important part of the synagogue, the 'ark' or 'tabernacle'.

A lamp always burns before the Jewish tabernacle. (If you go to a Catholic church, does this remind you of anything?)

(a) The Shema – the Law of God, summed up in a few words

Listen, Israel! the Lord is our God, the Lord is One.
You must love the Lord your God with all your heart,
and all your soul, and all your might.
The commandments I give you today
must be kept in your heart. *(Deuteronomy 6:4-5)*

(b) Psalm 72 – A prayer for the king to rule justly

O God, teach our king to be just,
and to judge people as you would judge.
May he rule over your people justly,
and see that the poor get their rights.
From the very hills and the mountains
may peace and justice rain down,
on all the poor and needy,
and drown those who oppress them.

(c) Jesus and the Jewish law

Jesus explained that the Jewish law was good. But Jesus improved on this law.

'Don't imagine that I have come to do away with the Law of Moses and the teaching of the prophets. I haven't come to do away with them, but to make their teachings come true.' *(Matthew 5:17)*

'You all know that the Law allows you to take "an eye for an eye". Well, I'm going even further. Take no revenge at all.' *(Matthew 5:38-39)*

'You all know that the Law forbids you to commit murder. Well, I say, "Don't even get angry with your neighbour"'. *(Matthew 5:21-22)*

(d) Helping others

Jesus said that the one thing we really have to do is to help others. He told a story about this. At the end of time everyone will gather around him, the Son of Man. He will separate the good people from the bad ones. He will say to the good people:

I was hungry and you fed me,
thirsty and you gave me a drink;
I was a stranger and you took me
into your home,
naked and you clothed me;
I was ill and you took care of me,
in prison and you visited me.

The good people will ask the Son of Man, *'When* was it that we saw *you* in need of help?'

He will reply: 'Whatever you did for one of the least important of these brothers and sisters of mine, you did for me.' *(From Matthew 25:34-40)*

(e) Treating others well

It isn't only followers of Jesus who believe that the greatest law is to treat others well:

> The ancient Chinese thinker Confucius said:
> 'Don't do to others what you don't want done to yourself.'

> The Jewish teacher Rabbi Hillel, who died when Jesus was your age, said:
> 'Don't do to anyone what you would hate being done to you.'

> Jesus put it the other way round:
> 'Do for other people what you would want them to do for you.'
> *(Matthew 7:12)*

> An Irish statesman, who died over 200 years ago, said:
> 'There is just one law for all, namely that law which governs all, the law of our Creator, the law of humanity, justice, equality – the law of nature, and of nations.' (Edmund Burke, 1729-97)

3. Outstanding examples from history and today

(a) St John Bosco – he showed that hard punishment did not make people obey laws. Kindness did

In England, and in other countries, people used to believe that the only way to treat people who broke the law, or behaved badly, was to give them severe punishments. Only 200 years ago, hungry people who stole a sheep were shipped off to Australia. Some were hanged. Today punishments are not so severe. Some people believe that young criminals should be treated more harshly today. St John Bosco would not agree.

John's father died when John was only 2 years old. His mother had a hard time bringing up her sons on their farm in Italy. Once when John was 9, he had a dream. He saw wild beasts turn into lambs, and disobedient children become well behaved. It made him think that it would be a good thing to help children. John became a priest. It was the early nineteenth century and a restless time in Europe. Many people moved to the towns, and this meant poverty and poor housing. Young boys got bored and became troublesome. Some were sent to prison.

John Bosco remembered his dream. He set up a home for the difficult boys and a remarkable thing happened. He won them all over with patience and kindness. He never punished them or got angry at bad behaviour. John was a great teacher who made religion and school work attractive because he gave his pupils time for sport and fun. He was always busy raising money to make his boys' homes comfortable, and to help the poor. (Many priests joined John and he soon had dozens of homes and schools. With the help of Mary Mazzarello, he also soon had many nuns caring for the girls.)

John Bosco believed that poverty and sickness often made people break laws. He proved that kindness and forgiveness is the best way to care for everyone, especially those who are troublesome.

St John Bosco's feast: 31 January.

(b) The Salvation Army – they care for people in all kinds of trouble

You have probably seen the Salvation Army in your town. Perhaps they were marching towards their meeting place, the Citadel, playing their band instruments. Or you may have seen them at Christmas, singing carols and collecting money. Who are they?

Their story began in Nottingham in the nineteenth century, with the birth of William Booth. William's father was a builder and the family were quite poor. As a youth William felt he must live a good life, following the example of Jesus. He became a Methodist (a member of a Christian Church), and then a preacher. When he married, his wife Catherine became a preacher too.

The young couple were worried that the Church seemed to ignore the poor. And there was much poverty. It was Victorian England, where cities were overcrowded and had slums. In 1862 William and Catherine left the Methodist Church, and, with their large family, moved to London. They began their *Christian Mission* in London's East End. It was a practical way of following the example and teaching of Jesus.

They went out to meet the poor. They fed the hungry, clothed the naked, cared for the sick and found homes for the homeless. Today William and Catherine's followers, all across the world, help the people who most need help: the homeless, prisoners, unmarried mothers, alcoholics, drug addicts and people searching for missing persons.

(c) St Luke – the doctor who cared about the sick and the poor

Can you imagine a world without doctors? They help us to keep healthy and, whenever they can, find ways to make us better. There have always been people who have wanted to make sick people well. One of the very early doctors that we know about is Luke. He was a doctor who travelled with St Paul on his long journeys. Then he wrote one of the four Gospels, telling us how he saw Jesus.

People who have read the four Gospels many times tell us that you can easily tell which of the four writers, Matthew, Mark, Luke or John, was the doctor. It is clearly Luke, because he most likes to tell stories about Jesus healing people and helping people who were outcasts. These outcasts were the sort of people that a doctor might have to visit. Other people would avoid them. In Jesus' time even women were 'outsiders'. Dr Luke tells quite a few stories about women. He tells us a lot about Jesus' mother, Mary.

Luke the doctor was not a Jew, so he probably never met Jesus. But he got enthusiastic about the stories he heard about him. Jesus was the very best sort of doctor, who could heal the sick and make unhappy people feel better.

(d) Mother Teresa – she cared for the poorest people

A few years ago a nun called Mother Teresa was known all over the world for her compassion for the poorest people in the world. She was once a geography teacher. She gave up her comfortable job in a smart girls' school in India, in order to live with very sick, dying and homeless people. A television programme was made about her work and everyone was amazed at the love she shared with the poor.

Some of her old pupils joined her, and then many young women from all over the world. They were a new order of nuns, called the Missionaries of Charity. A 'missionary' is someone who leaves home and travels a long way to spread good news, and 'Charity' is another word for 'love'. So Mother Teresa's sisters go out to spread the very good news that God loves everyone, especially poor and troubled people.

(e) Grace Darling – she risked her life for others

There are many people who help us and we never know their names. Some of their jobs can be very dangerous at times and they risk their lives for others: fire-fighters, paramedics (who drive ambulances), lifeboat people, and fishermen. The sea is a dangerous place to work. There is a famous story about a young lady who helped her father in the lighthouse. Her name was Grace Darling.

Grace grew up in a lighthouse because her father was the keeper on Browns-man Island, off the north-east coast of England. Grace was born in 1815. Her father taught all nine children to read and write, at home. And they helped with the lighthouse duties. By the time Grace was 19, only she and her 16-year-old brother stayed at home, helping on the lighthouse. She also made shirts for her brothers and mended fishing nets. She was a busy lady.

On 6 September 1838 there was a wild storm and a ship was smashed on the rocks. Grace helped her father prepare for the storm by bringing in the rabbit hutches and the washing basket. They lashed their small boat down and tied down its oars. Very early in the morning Grace saw the ship on the rocks. She and her father rowed out into the storm to rescue the nine survivors. The little boat could only carry seven. Grace rowed the boat in the mountainous seas as her father jumped onto the rocks to organise the survivors for the two journeys. Grace became a real heroine by risking her life to save others. Sadly she died only a few years later from tuberculosis, aged just 26.

4. Extra material

(a) Our first policemen

We first had policemen in early Victorian times, nearly 200 years ago. This was the time when towns became overcrowded because people moved in from the countryside. They thought they would get work. Instead there was terrible poverty and parts of the towns became slums. People turned to crime to live. The London slums were called 'The Devil's Acre'. Professional criminals called themselves 'Family People'. They were a sad, violent community who hated those who obeyed the law.

The criminals had their own pubs, 'flash houses', where they planned their crimes. And they had their own language:

a policeman – a 'crusher'   a pickpocket – a 'dibber'
a lookout – a 'crow'   get away quick – 'nommus'.
arrested – 'nibbed'

Charles Dickens wrote about this in *Oliver Twist*. The Artful Dodger was a 'dibber'.

In the 1800s there was no proper police force; law and order was kept by a few poorly paid officials working for the law courts. When there was serious trouble the army was called in. In 1829 Sir Robert Peel founded the London Metropolitan Police Force. They became known as 'bobbies' or 'peelers'. Later, other cities also founded a police force. Pictures of the 'peelers' show that they were dressed like servants, not soldiers. This was to show that they were to serve the community. And that is what they have always done.

(b) Jesus was a thoroughly Jewish boy

He was a Jewish child,
he had a Jewish nose,
he read the Jewish Bible
and wore all Jewish clothes.
He kept the Jewish Law
with Jewish thoroughness,
his Jewish mamma wouldn't let
her Jewish boy do less.
He loved the Jewish feasts,
the Jewish Temple too;
he prayed the Jewish psalter,
a proud and Jewish Jew. (Peter De Rosa)

(c) William Booth's battle cry for his Salvation Army

While women weep, as they do now,
I'll fight.
While children go hungry, as they do now,
I'll fight.
While men go to prison, as they do now,
I'll fight.
I'll fight to the very end.

(d) Sean Devereux – the UN worker who gave his life for others

Ten years ago our newspapers reported the death of a United Nations volunteer in the African country of Somalia. Sean was an energetic PE teacher from a Catholic secondary school in England. He volunteered to go to St Francis Salesian School in Liberia. He had always wanted to work for the poor, so he chose to teach boys who had very little. They loved him, and called him 'Mr Sean'. But war broke out in Liberia in 1990. Their happiness came to an end. To Sean's horror some of his pupils even became 'boy soldiers'.

Sean happened to be out of town, organising a sports day, when the fighting started, and he could not return to his school. He joined the United Nations relief workers and was fearless and courageous when he saw how badly the young soldiers were treated. He angered the military leaders by speaking out for the boys. He was beaten and imprisoned. Eventually Sean volunteered to go to the worst area of fighting, in Somalia. He joined UNICEF, the organisation that protected children.

Sean was horrified at the corruption in the army, and when he realised that the guns given to boy soldiers came from France, the USA and Britain, he spoke out against the authorities. They did not like it. His honesty and bravery cost him his life. One day he was shot in the head as he returned to quarters. He was killed to keep him quiet. Everyone who knew Sean was heartbroken at his death. He was only 28 years old.

5. Prayer and hymn

Prayer for all those who help us:
Our Father in heaven
you have shown us
in the life of Jesus, your Son,
that we are called to help each other.
We remember in our prayers today
all the people who help us
to live in safety and comfort.

We pray for nurses and doctors,
teachers and government ministers,
paramedics and firefighters,
police officers and shopkeepers,
our dinner staff and caretakers,
secretaries and cleaners.
And we pray especially for our parents
who help us every day to grow up
in safety and happiness. Amen.

Appropriate hymns:

 42 Brother, sister, let me serve you
 55 Come, Lord Jesus, come
311 Whatsoever you do

6. Suggestions for follow-up work

(a) Prepare a sheet of wallpaper (reverse side) on the wall for a frieze. Invite the pupils to write on the 'wall' the name or role of someone who helped them.

For example, 'The lollipop lady helped me across the road.'
'A doctor gave me some medicine to help me get better.'
'My mum helped me with my homework.'
Add to the 'wall' over the whole week.

(b) Invite the road safety officer, or a local police officer, into an assembly. Follow this up with a road safety quiz, in class or in a future assembly.

(c) Many groups of workers have 'patron saints'. Find out why the following saints have been chosen as patrons for:

Firefighters – St Florian (Feast, 4 May)
Police officers – St Michael (Feast, 29 September)
Nurses – St Camillus de Lellis (Feast, 14 July)
Teachers – St John Baptist de La Salle (Feast, 7 April)

7. Vocabulary

Police, teachers, fire officers, nurses, doctors, risk, rules, responsibility, safety.

5. Living in a diverse world
Unit 5 of Citizenship syllabus

1. Suggestions from the syllabus

(a) Our membership of different groups
(b) Respect for similarities and differences
(c) Differences of race and discrimination
(d) Prejudice and discrimination
(e) Diversity in local community
(f) Interdependence – worldwide

Introduction:

(a) Begin the assembly by having a look at the different groups that the children belong to. Activities will depend on the size of the assembly group. With a small group you could create some Venn Diagrams, showing the sizes and interaction between groups. Groups could be: 'children who live in the town', 'children who live in other areas', 'those who support the local football team', 'those who are in the scout or guide movement', 'children who are English', 'children who are Irish', 'children who are Italian', etc, . .

Alternatively, you could look at all the groups that exist in the school: children, adults, classes, teachers, other staff, the choir, the netball team, etc. . . .

(b) A piece of role play: Prepare a carefully chosen group of children to act out 'being exactly the same'.

They lead in, in step. Dressed in the same school uniform, same colour shoes, same hair style, holding same books, etc. They sit down together. You ask a question and they each put up the same hand, etc.

Ask the assembly, 'What is wrong?' (Everyone is the same, it is boring, awful.) How to change it? Get the 'actors' to change slightly – one girl could change her hairstyle, another could put a brightly coloured pencil case on her desk, etc.

Ask the assembly to imagine this on a larger scale:

everyone in the country dressed in brown;
everyone in the country eating the same meals;
everyone in the country supporting Manchester United . . .

Conclusion: Isn't it wonderful that we are all different?

(c) Make it something positive to be of a different race and religion. Prepare cards to be read out – if possible, use children from different racial and religious groups. If not, identify the 'actor' in an appropriate way, for example, a Jewish boy could wear a prayer shawl. The cards could read, for example: 'I am Teresa, my family come from Trinidad, in the West Indies. We have wonderful sunshine; we like sports and are good athletes and very good cricketers. We love to dance and sing. I look forward, every year, to the Carnival at Notting Hill, in London'. Make up other cards appropriate for your pupils.

(d) We all have an identity: 'I'm David, and I'm Jewish'; 'I'm Pauline and I'm English'; 'I'm Margaret, and I was born in Dublin'; 'I'm James and I am in the school first eleven'; . . . Invite the assembled children to think how they might describe themselves. Tell the children that it is *good* to be proud of who you are, and that it is really important that you accept that other people are different. No one has the right to 'look down' on another person, or make fun of them. Make large posters for display on the school corridors: 'PREJUDICE' *is not wanting others to be proud of who they are. It is not respecting them. Being different from others is* GOOD.' 'DISCRIMINATION *is behaving in a way that makes life difficult for another person.'*

(e) This part of the programme needs an assembly, and a follow-up, on its own.

Try and invite representatives of local churches, other faiths, other schools, etc. to the assembly. The local community groups you choose will depend on your locality. It would be good to include representatives of senior citizens' groups and playgroups. It would be especially 'productive' if you could invite children/staff from a school for children with special needs, and if you were in a position to invite asylum seekers. Let each class take one visitor back to their form base for a short while. Later, invite the pupils to suggest ways the diverse groups could come together occasionally to learn to appreciate each other.

(f) The worldwide community and interdependence. Have a large tray of food and other objects that are produced here and abroad. Hold them up and ask the pupils to identify where they originate: for example, banana, apple, chocolate bar, rubber, fork (Sheffield steel), gold chain, packet of tea, etc. Have cards prepared with the name of the countries where your objects come from and display these as they are identified. Explain that we need one another for survival.

Broaden the discussion to include, for example, foreign players in football teams; emergency rescue teams going from Britain to help in international disasters; VSO workers, and school leavers spending gap years in volunteer work abroad. (If your local secondary schools take part in this scheme invite someone to come to the assembly.)

2. Sacred writings: readings and reflections

(a) Exodus

> Do not deny justice to the poor when they appear in court. Do not make false accusations . . . Do not accept bribes, because a bribe makes people blind to what is right and ruins the case of those who are innocent. Do not ill-treat foreigners; you know how it feels to be a foreigner, because you were foreigners in Egypt. *(Exodus 23:6-9)*

(b) The Psalms

> How good it is, how wonderful,
> for people to live together in harmony! *(Psalm 133:1)*

(c) Zacchaeus

Retell the story of Zacchaeus from *Luke 19:1-10*.

Jesus was passing through the town of Jericho and crowds came out to see him.

Zacchaeus, a very rich and dishonest tax collector, was there. He was rather short and couldn't see over the crowds, so he climbed a tree. Jesus spotted him and invited him to get down because he would like to stay at his house. The crowd were really cross and grumbled about Jesus. Why? What kind of example was Jesus giving to us?

(d) The Good Samaritan

Retell the Parable of the Good Samaritan from *Luke 10:25-37*.

Emphasise that it was a story that Jesus told, using characters well known at that time. It may make the point better if you make it 'contemporary' and appropriate for your school. For example, for Norwich schools, the story could be: a Norwich City football fan on the way to the match at Carrow Road is mugged. A well-known dignitary and a Catholic headteacher pass by, in a rush to get to the game. A car driven by an Ipswich Town supporter stops and takes the victim to the hospital and misses the match. Who is the neighbour?

(e) The teaching of Islam

One of the important teachings of Islam is that people are not all the same, but they are all equal. Muslims believe that Allah created the whole of humankind from one soul and that their differences are intended:

> 'Among the signs given by Allah are the creation of the heavens and the earth, and the variations in languages and colours . . .' *(Surah 30:22)*

3. Outstanding examples from history and today

There are many examples of individuals who have worked to overcome prejudice and to build communities. The following are brief biographies.

(a) Fra Bartolome de las Casas

Most people in countries in South America speak Spanish. This is because over 500 years ago Spanish soldiers and Catholic missionaries sailed from Spain and took over the land in South America. They were quite ruthless in taking the land from the natives and in stealing their gold. It is a sad fact that the Church took part in this. However, one priest, called Fra Bartolome de las Casas, protested that they were wrong to be so cruel towards the local people. He was very concerned to help them and to treat them with dignity. He wrote: 'I have seen with my own eyes these gentle, peaceful people subjected to the most inhuman cruelties that have ever been committed . . . for no other reason than greed, the hunger and thirst for gold on the part of our own people.' The church authorities in Spain did not like to be told this; but today they realize that Fra Bartolome was right. They want him to be called a saint for having had the courage to speak out against the prejudice and racism of his own people.

(b) Elias Chacour

In the land where Jesus was born there is constant trouble. The Jewish people and the Arab (Palestinian) people both claim that they have the right to live there. Each side wants the other side to go away. There is prejudice and hatred on both sides. But one man stands out in his determination to bring the people together as one community. He is an Arab Christian, a Catholic priest called Elias Chacour. Elias grew up in the hills near where Jesus lived, and his parents taught him and his brothers and sisters to love the 'Man of Galilee' who had walked amongst the vineyards and olive groves of their hills. When Elias was 9, there was news that many Jews were returning to Palestine. (It was after the war.) His father said, 'This is wonderful news, we must be especially kind and make them feel at home.' Sadly, some prejudiced Jews came to the hills in Galilee and killed many of the Palestinians. Elias' father and brothers were taken prisoners. Elias' parents were quick to forgive the Jews, saying they had suffered much and needed sympathy, not hatred. When Elias grew up he remembered his mother's favourite words of Jesus: 'Blessed are the peacemakers'. He became a priest and in his little parish in the hills of Galilee he has built a large school and college where he invites Catholic, Jewish and Muslim children to study and live together. Fr Chacour is a brave man working quietly for peace and unity between races and religions.

(c) St Martin de Porres

Martin was born in Peru 400 years ago. His mother was an Indian and his father was from Spain. This made Martin a 'mulatto', a mixed-race child. We don't know if he ever suffered from prejudice or discrimination for being different from his friends. But the United States have named him the patron saint of those who work for unity and justice between people of different races. It is a very sad fact that many people treat people from other races badly. We call this racism. St Martin is a reminder that God created all people equal, whatever their race, colour or education.

Martin became a brother in a monastery, not a priest. This meant he took the simplest jobs, serving everyone else. But he did this so well, with such kindness, that local people began to go to him for help and advice, rather than to the priests or bishop. He was very much loved by everyone. Today we call him a saint because he did perfectly what Jesus taught: to love our neighbour and to serve them.

(d) Trevor Huddleston and Desmond Tutu

One of the countries in the world that has suffered most from racism and prejudice is South Africa. The native people are black, but the land was taken over by white people. This has been the cause of race hatred for many years. It became so bad that in recent times black South Africans were not allowed to vote; not allowed to have good schools; not allowed to travel on the good buses; not allowed to go into good shops. (You'll notice that the South African rugby team and cricketers are mostly white – because black children were not allowed to be trained with white children.)

An Anglican missionary priest, Fr Huddleston, was sent to South Africa and he was alarmed by this prejudice, and by the poverty of the black Africans. He also admired their patience and their dignity. He set out to speak up for them, especially to the government and the other South African authorities. One day he greeted a mother and her young son as they passed by in the street. They were amazed, because they were black. White people never spoke to them. The boy was called Desmond. He was so impressed that he asked to go to the school that Fr Huddleston ran for the local black community. He later became a priest, and today he is Archbishop Desmond Tutu. Trevor Huddleston died a few years ago. But he lived long enough to see a transformation in South Africa. His friend, Nelson Mandela, became the first black leader of the country and Desmond Tutu, who retired recently, led the Anglican Church in preaching about justice and forgiveness between the two races.

(e) Mohandas Gandhi

Mohandas was a very quiet, shy boy. His mother had to leave a light on in his room at night because he was frightened of ghosts and terrified of snakes. And there were many snakes in India, where Mohandas lived. At a very young age his parents arranged his marriage to Kasturbai. He decided to become a lawyer. India was ruled by Britain at the time, and Mohandas Gandhi came to England to study. This was in 1888.

Gandhi had realised that there were bad things wrong with the world, and he wanted his country to be free from the British. He was horrified when he went to work in South Africa to discover that Indian people there were treated like slaves. He spent the rest of his life struggling for change. Gandhi hated violence and racial and religious prejudice. The shy boy had become a bold young man. He told his Indian people to 'fight' the white government for their rights, but to 'fight' with love and respect. He hated violence and war.

Gandhi was a Hindu. The poorest Hindus were called 'untouchables' and given the dirty jobs. Gandhi would not accept that these poor families were less important than the rich ones. He called the 'untouchables' the 'children of God'. Gandhi said something very important: 'Hindus, Muslims, Christians – all should love each other and respect what the other person believes'. The quiet boy became famous, as a peace-loving man, who showed that peaceful actions can change the world. Sadly he was killed by a Hindu who didn't like to be told to live at peace with Muslims. Like Jesus, this good man died because he believed we are all the children of God.

(f) Janusz Korczak

During the Second World War, the Jewish people were treated appallingly by Hitler and the Nazis. Hitler wanted to get rid of all the Jews. At this time there was a Polish Jew, called Janusz Korczak, who worked as a doctor in Poland. He looked after the poor – especially orphaned children. He had two orphanages: one for Jewish children and one for non-Jewish children.

When the Nazis took over his country some friends offered to get him out of Poland, because all the Jews were being sent to prison camps. But Dr Korczak refused to leave his Jewish orphans. In 1942, he and his staff, and all 200 children, were marched three miles to the 'deportation train'. He led them, holding two children's hands in his. They were all gassed at a terrible death camp, called Treblinka. This wonderful, courageous man gave up his life for the children. He firmly believed that all of us are loved as children of God.

4. Extra material

(a) There is a great deal of prejudice in Israel today. This is the land where Jesus lived. It is shared by Arabs and Jews, but many people do not want to share. Some Arab children grow up hating the Jewish children. And some of the Jewish children are taught to hate the Arab children. Recently a Jewish student who was from Scotland went to Israel. He was on a bus when a bomb, set off by Arabs, exploded, and he was killed. The young man had left a message that if he died (he knew he was in a dangerous place) he would like to become a donor – leave parts of his body to save the life of someone else. (This is called 'organ transplants'.) He said he did not mind if the very sick person was a Palestinian Arab or a Jew. The doctors read his message and transplanted a part of his body to save the life of a little Palestinian girl. A young Jewish student saved the life of an Arab child.

(b) A poem by a young Jewish boy, living in Israel:

> I don't like wars,
> they end up with monuments.
> I don't want battles to roar,
> even in neighbouring continents.
>
> I like spring,
> flowers producing,
> fields covered with green,
> the wind in the hills whistling.
>
> Drops of dew I love,
> the scent of jasmine as night cools,
> stars in darkness above,
> and rain singing in pools.
>
> I don't like wars. They end
> in wreaths and monuments;
> I like Peace come to stay
> and it will some day. (Matti Yosef, 9 years)

(c) If your local football team has a policy about stamping out racism in football, it may be possible to invite someone from the club to talk at assembly.

(d) Your town or city is probably twinned with a town or city abroad. This may be the opportunity to explore the links.

5. Prayer and hymn

> Our Father in heaven,
> you are a God who delights in difference:
> you made valleys as well as mountains,
> dry deserts as well as fountains,
> ladybirds and ants
> as well as elephants,
> dark as well as light
> day as well as night,
> hot as well as cold,
> the surprising new as well as the old.

You made some of us tall
and some of us short,
some of us dark
and some of us fair.
There are those with auburn curls,
and those with straight black hair.
Help us to embrace them all as you do
and to realise each day more deeply
what a dull world this would be
if we were all the same. Amen.

Appropriate hymns:

  13 All God's people, come together
  83 Give me peace, O Lord, I pray
135 I'm black, I'm white, I'm short, I'm tall
168 Kum ba yah, my Lord
313 When I needed a neighbour

6. Suggestions for follow-up work

(a) Place a world map on the classroom wall. Ask the pupils to bring labels from tins of food, tea, coffee, etc. and pin them around the map locating where they come from. Build this up over a few weeks.

(b) Make another frieze to illustrate the major world religions. Set this around a world map to show the spread of the religions. Build this up over a few weeks with colourful illustrations, postcards, etc.

(c) Make a school/class photo album to show the different groups who work together to make up the school community.

7. Vocabulary

Identity, community, responsibility, environment, connections, race, racism, religion, language, diversity, culture, interdependence, tolerance, respect.

6. Developing our school grounds
Unit 6 of Citizenship syllabus

1. Suggestions from the syllabus

(a) Needs of people
(b) Needs of all living things
(c) Use of resources to develop local environment
(d) Wildlife
(e) Care for local environment/world environment

Introduction

One way to introduce this topic (and the next) would be the UN statements on the Human Rights of the Child – as explained to children by UNICEF (there is a leaflet that suggests the responsibilities that go with the rights). A selection of the rights and responsibilities could be written on posters and displayed in the school corridors this week. For example:

'If every child has a right to be protected from conflict and cruelty, then they also have a responsibility not to bully or harm each other.'

'If children have a right to a clean environment then they also have a responsibility to do what they can to look after their environment.'

(a) The posters could be shown to illustrate the needs that all children have. This week in the assembly, use the poster that emphasises the need for recreation, space and a pleasant environment. Show pictures of children who are denied this (use CAFOD, Christian Aid or UNICEF material. They will send you posters).

(b) Explain to the children that most people in the world have respect for the animal world (perhaps refer back to Unit 3, page 17). This is because many people have a religious faith and believe that God, or Allah, created all living things. Scientists, even those who don't believe in God, have a sense of wonder at the extraordinary world of animal, bird and insect life. In recent years people have become much more concerned about the needs of all living things; that they should be allowed to live in harmony alongside human beings. We are going to look at our school grounds to see how we can improve this.

(c) Human beings can create ugly, dangerous environments. Usually this happens when towns are built hurriedly, industry is only concerned with making profit, and people don't plan carefully – thinking only of their own interests.

But careful planning and concern for the whole environment can mean that beautiful environments can be created or preserved. Perhaps you could start a survey of your school grounds at this point. Give the classes some specific tasks, something to investigate, for example: Which class can identify the most insects, birds, etc. that come into your grounds?

(d) Make suggestions to the assembled children about the kind of wildlife that could exist in either an urban or country environment (according to the location of your school).

There are many environmental agencies that could be contacted. Libraries usually have leaflets about local groups. Ask for a representative from one of these groups to come to the assembly and offer advice.

(e) The work of your local environmental groups could be 'advertised' in your school on a noticeboard and described in a few words at your assembly. Examples will vary across the country. For example, in the Norwich area the following groups could be contacted for material:

The National Council for the Conservation of Plants and Gardens (Norfolk Group)

The Norfolk Conservation Corps ('Do something practical for Nature in Norfolk')

The RSPB

Norfolk Biodiversity Partnership

Norfolk Wildlife Trust

British Trust for Conservation Volunteers

English Nature (Norfolk Nature newsletter)

Assemblies are an opportunity to remind the pupils of our responsibility to create a pleasant and safe environment for our neighbours. Two examples: litter and rubbish; fouling of streets by dogs.

Some attention should be given to the worldwide environment, especially noting how human beings can be very destructive when they think only of profit, ignoring our responsibility for future generations, and for the whole of creation. Examples could be the destruction of the rainforests, and the ozone layer; pollution in general – from cars, from agricultural waste into the river systems, etc. This may be tied in with geography or literacy programmes.

2. Sacred writings: readings and reflections

(a) Genesis

Then God commanded, 'Let the earth produce every kind of plants, those that bear seed and those that bear fruit' – and it was done. So the earth produced all the different kinds of plants, and God was pleased with what he saw. (Genesis 1:11-12)

Then God placed the man in the Garden of Eden to cultivate it and take care of it. *(Genesis 2:15)*

(b) The Psalms

O God, it is right for us to praise you,
and to keep our promises to you . . .
You care for the land by sending rain,
and making it rich and fertile.
You fill its streams with water;
and provide the earth with crops.

You shower your rain on the ploughed fields
and soak them with water;
you soften the soil with showers
to let the young plants grow.
What a rich harvest you provide in your goodness! *(Psalm 65:1-11)*

(c) Noah

You could tell the story of Noah in your own words (Genesis 9:1-17). Emphasise God's promise to protect his animals, birds and all living things. Point out that this needs our co-operation. We are the ones to do this for him.

(d) Jesus' nature parables

Jesus used parables in his teaching; stories with a meaning. Many of the stories he told were about the countryside: a mustard seed, a sower, a fig tree. He told a kind of parable about himself. He called himself a Good Shepherd.

I am a good shepherd, willing to die for my sheep. When the hired man, who isn't a full-time shepherd and doesn't own the sheep, sees a wolf coming, he leaves the sheep and runs. The hired man runs for it because he's only a hired man and doesn't care about the sheep. I am a good shepherd. I know my sheep and they know me. And I'm willing to die for them.
(John 10:11-15)

Use the story to show how we look after what belongs to us. Our school is 'ours'. We must look after it, keep it beautiful, including the grounds.

(e) Harvest Festival

This could be the time to prepare for a school harvest festival. Each autumn Christians celebrate the richness of creation with a festival. They give thanks and praise for the food we can grow. Churches and Christian schools very often use this occasion to help the less fortunate by donating food for the poor in their district.

Catholic schools may want to link this with the CAFOD fast days.

Other schools may link this with Christian Aid week in May.

Pupils could decorate the hall or classroom with greenery from the grounds.

(f) The Jewish Festival of Sukkot

Jews, worldwide, remember that they are dependent on God for their food and protection. The feast lasts eight days. It is also their harvest thanks-giving. Families build a temporary shelter, covered in branches and leaves. It is to remind them of the 40 years their ancestors spent in the desert. God provided their food, the Manna.

> Every year you must celebrate three festivals in my honour. In the month of Abib (March-April), the month when you left Egypt, you must cele-brate the Festival of Unleavened Bread as I taught you . . . At the time of the first wheat harvest, you must celebrate the Harvest Festival. And in the autumn, when you have harvested the last of your crops, you must cele-brate the Festival of Sukkot (Tents). *(Exodus 23:14-16)*

3. Outstanding examples from history and today

(a) Chico Mendes

Francisco 'Chico' Mendes was a rubber-tapper in north-west Brazil. He had never been to school, because he began work at 9 years old. The land-owners would not let the poor people learn to read or write, because they could then cheat them in their wages. In the 1960s cattle ranchers bought the rubber estates – to make more pasture for cattle. Chico's family had a very hard time. They saw their forests cut down and the land ruined. But one day an educated man met Chico. They became friends and he taught Chico to read, and he spoke to him about the rights of workers. Chico founded a group called the Alliance of the People of the Forest. He led peaceful protests against the landowners who were destroying the forests. But Chico was shot dead in front of his wife and children in 1988. They wanted to shut him up. His wife said: 'When Chico died I was filled with despair, but God comforted me and inspired me to carry on his work.' Which she does today.

(b) St Hildegard

A very long time ago, over 900 years ago, a girl called Hildegard was born. She had nine older brothers and sisters. When she was 8 she was sent away to school to be looked after and taught by a lady called Jutta. Jutta taught Hildegard all about God and his beautiful world. The little girl never forgot this and always said that the world was 'lit up by God'. Later Hildegard became a nun so that she could spend all her time thinking about this. And she did just that. We know all about her because she became a great writer, poet and musician. She wrote two books on natural history, and many poems about the world of nature as she saw it in the hillside and the river valley where she lived. She praised God for all living things on earth, the mountains, fields, rivers, plants and trees. Her music is still played, and is now on CD. Perhaps you could write a song about creation.

(c) Jewish beliefs

The Jews have always had a great sense of responsibility for the environment. This is based on their belief that God created the world, and made human beings to take care of it. Psalm 24:1 says: 'The world, and all it holds, belongs to God.'

Jews believe that God scattered divine sparks (his presence) throughout the whole world. It is the task of human beings to reunite the world in harmony, by caring for the environment. This is called *Tikkun Olam*. Rabbi Hertzberg said, 'The rebirth of nature, day after day, is a gift of God; but humans are responsible for making sure that this rebirth can take place.'

In the Torah, it is said that trees are not to be destroyed, even in war (Deuteronomy 20:19). Trees have been important to the Jews since they rebuilt Israel in 1948. The land is like a desert in parts, and the soil was constantly being blown away. *The Jewish National Fund* organised a programme to plant millions of trees to bring life back to the soil. After the terrible treatment of the Jews by Hitler, a memorial was built in Jerusalem to remember the millions who were killed. Trees were planted at this place, Yad Vashem. One row of trees remembers the good Gentiles (non-Jews), who helped the Jews at this time.

Many people go to Israel, from all over the world, to help develop the land. They live in communities, called *Kibbutzim*, where the land is restored to grow vegetables and fruit. The workers have also built 280 nature reserves. The Jews are very good environmentalists.

(d) Muslim beliefs

Muslims believe that God (Allah) made the world, and that human beings have been given the responsibility to look after it. They call this *khalifah*. The pattern of the universe is fixed and balanced. Humans must always keep this balance by considering the needs of *all* creation.

The first Muslims lived in the desert where water was scarce. This is why Muslims consider water to be the most precious gift from God. Once the Prophet Muhammad set his followers an example. They were on a long, hot journey, and came to a stream. The Prophet's friends jumped into the water, but Muhammad took a small bowl from his bag and took only a little water to wash himself. He told his friends that Allah gave us water as a gift, and we should never waste it.

4. Extra material

(a) Canticle of the Sun by St Francis of Assisi

> O most high, almighty and good Lord God,
> to you be praise, glory, honour and blessing.
> Praise to you, my Lord, for all your creatures,
> especially for Brother Sun
> who brings us the day and the light;
> how beautiful he is, and with what splendour he shines.
> Praise to you, my Lord, for Sister Moon,
> and for all the stars so bright in the heavens.
> Praise to you, my Lord, for Sister Water,
> so precious, so clean, and so humble.
> Praise to you, my Lord, for Sister Earth
> who sustains us and delights us with her many fruits,
> and her coloured flowers and the grass.

(b) This is an opportunity to show or display paintings of gardens, flowers, trees, etc. The work of Monet could be a good example. Monet's garden could inspire some art work from the pupils.

(c) This is also an opportunity to talk about sensory gardens for the blind. Ask the children to suggest what should be included; how it should be arranged.

(d) Collect (in advance of the assemblies) local newspaper cuttings about work for the environment.

Examples:

(i) A young girl in Norwich was bullied and treated badly by a group of local boys. She faced the problem, with help from family and school, and resolved to do something about it. She believed that the boys were bored so she started a successful campaign to have a local field given to the young people of her village, for their recreation.

(ii) Most parts of the country have conservation groups. Activities are sometimes reported in the local press, and many involve young people helping in the work.

5. Prayer and hymn

(a) The Canticle of the Sun (see above)

(b) The CAFOD prayer for the harvest

> Generous God
> lead me in your ways
> and know me,
> guide me on your paths.

Lead me to your truth
and teach me,
show me to care.
Giving God,
may all people
who turn to you in hope,
sing for joy
while the smiles of your children
shine like the sun
at harvest time. Amen.

Appropriate hymns:

   5 All creatures, bless the Lord
   6 All creatures of our God and King
  22 All the nations of the earth
170 Laudato sii, O mi Signore
306 We plough the fields and scatter

6. Suggestions for follow-up work

(a) An inter-class competition to discover how many insects, animals, plants, trees and flowers can be seen in the school grounds.

(b) Using the vocabulary below, role-play with your class a planning committee to redesign the school grounds.

(c) Create a new corner in the grounds, with the help of parents and children. For example, a butterfly bed.

(d) Let the pupils write their own psalms, praising God for all they found in their school grounds – see (a) above – illustrate them in the way the monks illustrated the illuminated manuscripts.

7. Vocabulary

Environment, features, facilities, playground, locality, place, planning, discussion, democracy, consultation, negotiation, communication.

7. Children's rights – human rights

Unit 7 of Citizenship syllabus

1. Suggestions from the syllabus

(a) Difference between needs, wants and rights
(b) Rights with responsibilities – support others in their quest for rights
(c) Honesty, trust, tolerance and respect for others
(d) UN Convention on the Human Rights of the Child
(e) Caring about other people's feelings
(f) Understanding consequences of racism, teasing, aggression and bullying
(g) Human rights issues in the news/history

Introduction

(a) You could begin this assembly by filling in, with the children, three charts: NEEDS, WANTS and RIGHTS. They will have discussed this with you earlier in Units 2 and 3. Read again some of the UNICEF rights for children (Unit 6).

(b) This could lead into a discussion of our responsibility to share with other children. It would be helpful to have a video programme of children in the developing world, showing their needs. CAFOD, Christian Aid, Tear Fund, UNICEF, etc. could provide these. At the time of an international disaster, flooding, earthquake, etc. there is probably TV news material that would help the children appreciate their need to help others. (The children's television programme, *Newsround,* is helpful).

(c) Honesty, trust, tolerance and respect for others. To ensure the children understand these words and concepts, create a few situations, appropriate to your school, that illustrate them. For example, you are collecting sweets to give to a local charity for Christmas. You are going to pick a group of children to be in charge of the collection. You must be able to *trust* them to be *honest*.

(d) UN Convention on the Human Rights of the Child. It is likely that there is a UNICEF partnership group in your neighbourhood. One of the group may be able to come to an assembly to talk about this, and to bring posters etc. On the first Friday in February, UNICEF hold a national non-uniform day, for the world's disadvantaged children. They send out colourful and detailed project material for the year's cause. This could be a useful introduction to the unit.

(e) Caring about other people's feelings. Some role play could be useful. Have several small groups of children on the platform. Each group, in turn, gossips and makes fun of another group or individual. Topics could be: elderly people walking slowly along the road; the boy who has old, non-cool trainers; the girl who doesn't know the latest pop group in the news; the new immigrant boy who cannot speak English very well. Discuss with the assembled children how the people would feel if they overheard the remarks. How could you make all the people in your examples feel welcomed?

(f) Extend your discussion (above) to include victims of racism, teasing, aggression and bullying. This is a good time to evaluate the workings of your bullying policy.

(g) Keep a lookout for human rights issues in the news at this time, and if appropriate talk about them. Not all issues would be appropriate for this age group, but our children would understand the injustices that other children suffer. For example, child sweat labour. It was young children in India who spent hours in factories sewing the footballs used in the World Cup. CAFOD, Christian Aid, UNICEF, Save the Children, etc. will give you information.

2. Sacred writings: readings and reflections

(a) The prophet Amos

The prophet Amos preached to the people of northern Israel at a time when they were prosperous. Everything seemed comfortable and safe. But the prophet saw that the rich people were getting richer by oppressing the poor. This made their religious observances false. He spoke out passionately and with courage, warning the people that God would punish them for their injustice to the poor.

> Why are you so afraid of bringing wrongdoers to court, and of speaking the whole truth? Why do you continue to tax the poor, and rob them of their grain? I warn you: those fine stone houses you have built for yourselves will be yours no longer. That fine wine from the beautiful vineyards you have planted will be yours no longer . . . You, who persecute the innocent, and fake bribes, and prevent the poor getting justice in court . . . Start doing what is right, not what is wrong. Your lives depend on it. *(Amos 5:10-14)*

(b) The prophet Isaiah

> The kind of fasting I want is this: Remove the chains of oppression and the yoke of injustice, and let the oppressed go free. Share your food with the hungry and open your homes to the homeless poor. Give clothes to those who have nothing to wear, and do not refuse to help your own relatives.
>
> *(Isaiah 58:6-7)*

(c) Jesus blesses the children

Some people brought children to Jesus for him to place his hands on them and pray for them. The disciples tried to stop them. But Jesus said, 'Let the children come. Don't stop them, because the Kingdom of Heaven belongs to such as these.' *(Matthew 19:13-14)*

(d) Jesus heals a man who was an outcast

Jesus was in a town where there was a man suffering from a dreaded skin disease. When he saw Jesus, he threw himself down and begged him, 'Sir, if you want to, you can heal me.'

Jesus stretched out his hand and touched him. 'I do want to,' he answered. 'Be healed!' At once the disease left him. *(Luke 5:12-13)*

(e) A parable of Jesus

Jesus told a story (parable) about a great feast.

A wealthy man decided to have a great party. He invited all his friends, but to his surprise, they all seemed to have other things to do. They all made excuses for not attending. The man was upset, in fact quite angry. So he sent out his servant to go into the streets and invite a whole number of people, and those who were usually left out, to come to the party. The homeless, the unemployed, the asylum seekers and the ex-prisoners all went to the party and enjoyed themselves. *(Luke 14:15-24)*

Jesus said that the Kingdom of God is like this party. What did he mean?

3. Outstanding examples from history and today

(a) The Earl of Shaftesbury (Anthony Ashley Cooper)

Ashley was born over 200 years ago. He lived in the Victorian times when the streets of the large cities were dirty and crowded. He was distressed at the sight of children working hard to earn a few pennies. His family were Evangelical Anglicans and they were anxious to help the poor families. They knew that this is what Jesus would have done. Ashley became a Member of Parliament when he was 25 years old, and 25 years later he succeeded his father as the Earl of Shaftesbury and went into the House of Lords.

He will always be remembered for his work at Westminster. He kept on and on working to help improve the lives of the poor, especially the children. He was successful in improving housing conditions and building schools for the poor. He made Parliament change the laws about working conditions for children. In Victorian times they had to work in coal mines and climb inside chimneys to sweep them. But he put a stop to this. Unfortunately, many children in other parts of the world still have to work in terrible conditions today. They need someone like Lord Shaftesbury to speak up for them.

(b) Archbishop Oscar Romero

Oscar Romero was born in El Salvador, Central America, in 1917. He was a quiet boy, who worked hard at school and led a fairly comfortable life. He became a Catholic priest, and was then made a bishop. El Salvador is a strange country, because the land is owned by just a few very rich families. The rest are dreadfully poor, and the rich will not share with their poor neighbours. Bishop Romero was made the archbishop of the capital city, San Salvador, when the country was in great trouble. He could have lived a comfortable life, in a fine house as a friend of the rich.

Instead, like the prophet Amos, he spoke out against the selfishness and injustice of the rich and powerful people. He spoke out about the rights of the poor and the responsibility of the wealthy to help them. He said that this is what the Gospel demanded. He was told to be quiet, but he kept on reminding the politicians to work for *all* the people. He was finally silenced when someone shot him dead, while he was saying Mass. Christians call him a martyr, because he died following the example of Jesus.

(c) Martin Luther King

Racism is one of the worst injustices in the world. Christians believe that God made everyone to be equal. In many parts of the world, in the past and still today, some people are treated as though they are not equal to others. Many years ago African slaves were taken across the seas to the southern states of the USA, to work in the cotton fields. They were treated badly, even after President Abraham Lincoln ended slavery in 1863. Black American children were not allowed to go to school with white children. Their parents could not travel on the bus, or go into restaurants with white people.

Fifty years ago, Martin Luther King Junior, a black Baptist minister, began to work for equal human rights for his people. He had a difficult time because he insisted on protesting peacefully. He refused to use violence, even when his family received death threats. His house was bombed, he was stabbed and imprisoned. He continued to preach forgiveness and love, insisting that all people are equal and deserve to be treated the same, with respect and fairness. He was shot dead in Memphis, Tennessee, by those who disagreed with him. He is thought of by the Christian community as a prophet and a martyr.

(d) Eglantyne Jebb and Save the Children Fund

Eglantyne was born into an extraordinary Christian family, in 1876. Her father was a landowner and well educated. He started a debating society (a group meeting to discuss important issues) in his home. The children, the servants and the farm workers were all invited to join. Her mother was keen to make the servants' and workers' lives more interesting, so she gave them lessons in painting, wood carving, basket-making, and even carpentry.

Eglantyne was one of the first women to go to Oxford University. She loved it, studying hard, dancing, rowing and playing hockey. She became a teacher, but didn't enjoy it very much. In 1912 there was a war in Europe, the Balkan War. It changed Eglantyne's life. She joined some of her family in northern Greece who were offering help to the thousands of war refugees. Eglantyne was shocked to find so many children dying of starvation and sickness. The British Consul asked her to help, so she returned to England and began to raise money to save the children's lives.

With her sister Dorothy, Eglantyne founded Save the Children Fund. It was not an easy task – she was even prosecuted for giving out leaflets showing starving babies. But people did come to her help, especially Pope Benedict XV, who asked the Catholic Church to support her. Then the leaders of the Anglican, Orthodox and Free Churches joined in the appeals. The Children's Fund fed and housed refugee children, and set up schools and hospitals and homes for disabled children. Eglantyne worked tirelessly for the poor for the rest of her life, in Russia, the Balkans, Africa, India and China. Above all she fought for the rights of children to be recognised. In 1924, the League of Nations accepted her 'Children's Charter'.

When she died at the age of 52, those who knew her called her 'a saint', a lovely woman who had wanted to live a quiet life of prayer, but felt she *had* to work to help children in need.

(e) Muslim relief

For Muslims, one of the names of Allah is 'The Compassionate'. They believe that this means they too must show compassion to anyone who is suffering. Muslims have an international relief agency, called Islamic Relief. It was set up in 1984 to raise money for earthquake and flood victims. Later, money was raised to help the victims of war in Bosnia and Somalia. Muslims have always given generously to help children, especially orphans and victims of wars and disasters. When a new-born baby is named, gifts are given to the family, called *Aqiqah*. Very often the family will give some of this money to help poorer children.

(f) Jewish relief

The Jewish people are well known for helping one another. From a very early age children are encouraged to give some of their pocket money to help the poor. They have charity money boxes, called *pushkes*, in their homes. Giving help to the poor is called *Tzedaka* (Justice). Jews believe that everything we have really belongs to God, and so we have to share it with others, who are in need. Every Friday evening as the Sabbath begins, Jews are expected to give money to charities.

Jewish children are taught to be kind to others and to show compassion for anyone who is suffering. This is called *Gemilut Hasidim*. They are reminded that their famous rabbi Maimonides said the best thing to give is not money, but your time to help others. The Jews have a Feast called Yom Kippur when they fast (go without food) for 24 hours. It is to help them understand how it feels to be hungry.

4. Extra material

(a) Martin Luther King's dream.

Martin Luther King made a famous speech, 'I have a dream', before he died. He dreamt of a world where his four young children would be judged by their behaviour and attitudes, not by the colour of their skin.

(b) The first Declaration of the Rights of the Child
(written by Eglantyne Jebb in 1924 in Geneva.)

- The child must be given the means to develop materially and spiritually.
- The hungry child must be fed; the sick child nursed; the backward child developed; the delinquent child helped; and the orphan looked after.
- The child must be the first to receive help in times of distress.
- The child should be prepared for work, and never exploited.
- The child must be taught that talents should be used for the service of others.

The work of UNICEF (the United Nations Children's Fund)
UNICEF is an organisation devoted to improving the lives of children across the world. It is a part of the United Nations, which tries to keep peace worldwide. The main purpose of UNICEF is to make sure all children can grow into happy, healthy adults.

In 1989, the United Nations General Assembly accepted the 'Convention on the Rights of the Child'. It includes the following rights:

- healthcare
- education
- a fair standard of living
- leisure and play
- protection from exploitation and abuse
- expression of opinions.

A typical report from a UNICEF worker in the African Ivory Coast

More than 30,000 young girls work as maids in rich families. Poor families send their young daughters away from home to earn money. (Some are only 9 years old.) They work more than 70 hours a week for about £3. They don't have health care or any protection. We are working with a Catholic organisation to improve the girls' lives. We have begun an education programme for them, and this means the employers have to give them two afternoons a week free. When we organised a workshop on children's rights for agencies that recruit the maids, they were stunned when we told them that children have rights. They call them 'slaves'.

And when we told the children that they had rights, they did not believe us. Now they know that they can have a work contract, a better salary and some time off.

5. Prayer and hymn

Our Father in heaven,
we ask you today
to be with us as we pray for other children.
Help us to understand the needs
of children who live in countries where food is scarce,
or where neighbours are at war with each other.
Help us to open our hearts to all children
who are sick or dying,
to those who are orphans or in need,
to those who are injured by landmines or bombs.
Help us to understand
that ours are the only hands
that you have got to help them.
We ask this in the name of Jesus
whose heart went out to all those in need. Amen.

Appropriate hymns:

  35 Bind us together, Lord
  73 Feed us now, O Son of God
 111 He's got the whole world in his hands
304 We have a dream

6. Suggestions for follow-up work

(a) Invite a representative from CAFOD or Christian Aid or Save the Children Fund, to come to your school for the morning. Link this with an opportunity to raise money for them, for example, Family Fast Day, Children in Need, or Christian Aid Week.

(b) Take part in the UNICEF Make a Change Day, on the first Friday of February. Schools are invited to have a non-uniform day to raise money for a specific UNICEF project. The project will be centred around education for children in the developing world. Some projects target the Street Children.
(See appendix for contact addresses.)

(c) Invite the children to write a poem about their dream for a future world: 'I have a dream'.
Display the poems and offer a prize.

7. Vocabulary

Human rights, responsibilities, fairness, charter.

8. How do rules and laws affect me?

Unit 8 of Citizenship syllabus

1. Suggestions from the syllabus

(a) Research topical issues, problems about rules, etc.
(b) How and why rules are made and enforced
(c) Why rules are needed; how to shape them
(d) Consequences of anti-social behaviour (bullying, racism, vandalism) on individuals and communities
(e) Democracy; parliament; leaders

Introduction

If you are following these assembly ideas in order, then you will have already discussed the need for rules, and the consequences of breaking them. For a revision of this, turn to Unit 4.

(a) Topical issues are suggested as the way to introduce the problems with rules. If none is appropriate, perhaps a useful way for children to understand the need for rules would be to analyse games of football and netball. Let the staff responsible for PE address the assembly, and talk about the rules of the games. They could tell the pupils how difficult it is to umpire or referee a game. Are there occasions when they think it best to let a rule be broken? Why should the referee's decision be final? Can he/she make mistakes?

(b) When a group work together they must respect each other. Without rules of behaviour it seems, from experience, that this doesn't happen. With everyone obeying the same rules, people feel they are treated fairly. All ancient civilisations made their rules of behaviour, and set up authorities to see they were observed. You could retell the story of Moses receiving the Ten Commandments.

(c) Why rules are needed. Have a group of children on the platform playing board games. Let one group ignore the rules, and start arguing loudly: 'I don't want to start with a 6; 'No, I had to miss a go last time, I'm not going to now'; 'I'm having another go, I only had a 1 last time'. Ask some questions: It is a rule that you give in your homework on the day your teacher says. Why?

It is a traffic rule that you observe the traffic lights. Why?

It is a crime in law to shoplift. Why?

(d) Bullying, racism and vandalism are issues constantly in the national and local press. It may be an idea to focus on some of these actual occurrences. Outline the incident; show its consequences on the individual and/or community. These issues can be included in a discussion on the Commandment, 'Thou shalt not steal'. Bullying and racism steal a person's self-confidence and happiness. Vandalism is stealing an individual's property or the community's pleasant environment. It is selfishness.

(e) **Leadership:**
Give examples of good leaders and bad leaders.

Good leaders:	*Bad leaders:*
• Listen to others	• Never listen to others
• Work with others	• Ignore others
• Use resources wisely	• Waste resources
• Know they get it wrong sometimes	• Believe they are always right
• Think of the needs of others	• Think of themselves

Democracy:
When a country is led by one person who has all the power and no one else to listen to, it is very often a disaster. If the king, or ruler, has very little concern for the people, everyone suffers. To prevent this happening, a form of government was developed, called 'democracy'. It means that everyone in the country can be involved. Our country is a democracy. The people can vote for representatives to speak for them in Parliament. The leader of the country (prime minister) is chosen by the people. The prime minister leads one 'party'. There are several different 'parties', so that people have a choice of different ways of thinking about government. It is having a CHOICE that makes a democracy.

Parliament:
In London, our representatives meet to discuss how to run the country. They are called Members of Parliament (MPs). They meet in a building called the Houses of Parliament at Westminster, alongside the River Thames. The MPs meet to see if the rules of the country are working well. Sometimes they vote to change them. For example, there is a rule that allows fox-hunting in the countryside. Many people do not like this, so the MPs will vote to see if they should change the law and stop it. Scotland and Wales now have their own form of government, independent of England.

2. Sacred writings: readings and reflections

It would perhaps be appropriate at this point to talk about the Kingdom of God. Christians have their own very special leader in Jesus. He showed us that we belong to two kingdoms, an earthly one and the Kingdom of God. The Kingdom of God is also found on earth. People 'live' in this kingdom when they live in the way Jesus taught. That is, when they love one another, forgive one another and help one another.

(a) The Psalms

The Jewish people, Jesus included, loved God's law. They often sang about it in the Psalms.

> How I love your law!
> I think about it all day long.
> Your commandments are always in my mind,
> and make me wiser than my enemies.
> I understand more than all my teachers,
> because I meditate on all your instructions. *(Psalm 119:97-99)*

Praising God as the Supreme King.

> The Lord is mighty in Zion;
> he is supreme over all the nations.
> Everyone will praise
> his great and awesome name.
> The Lord is holy.
> You love what is good, O mighty king.
> You have established justice in Israel;
> you have shown us what is right and fair.
> Praise the Lord our God,
> worship before his throne!
> Our God is holy! *(Psalm 99:2-5)*

(b) King Solomon's prayer

David is remembered as the great king of Israel, who ruled on behalf of God. When David died his son Solomon became the new king. He asked God to help him. This was his prayer:

> O Lord God, you have let me succeed my father as king, even though I don't really know how to rule, because I am very young. There are so many people in this kingdom of yours. Please give me the wisdom I am going to need to rule your people with justice. I need to know the difference between good and evil. *(1 Kings 3:7-9)*

Solomon did become a wise king. There is a story that shows how wise he was. Two women, living in the same house, had babies at the same time. One baby died and both the mothers claimed that the living baby was theirs. They went to the king to ask for his judgement. Each mother said, 'The baby is mine.' Solomon sent for a sword and said, 'Cut the living child in two and give half to each mother.' The real mother cried out, 'No, let her have the baby', but the other mother said, 'Neither of us will have it; cut it in two.' Immediately the king knew that the real mother was the one who would not let the baby be killed. He gave her the baby.

(c) Jesus and the law

The Gospels record an occasion when Jesus was asked a trick question by some people who criticised his teaching. They wanted an 'either/or' answer: Should we obey the laws of the land or God's law? Jesus said, 'Obey both.' *(Mark 12:13-17)*

(d) The Sermon on the Mount

Matthew gives a detailed account of Jesus' teaching about the Law. This is in what we call 'The Sermon on the Mount'. *(Matthew 5-7)*

Jesus said: 'Don't imagine that I have come to do away with the Law of Moses and the teachings of the prophets . . . I've come to make their teachings come true.' *(Matthew 5:17)*

Jesus showed that sometimes laws, even the sacred Jewish Torah, needed to be improved. He said, for example: 'You all know that the Law forbids you to commit murder. Well, I say, "Don't even get angry with your neighbour." You all know that the Law allows you to take "an eye for an eye, and a tooth for a tooth". Well, I'm going further. Take no revenge at all. If someone hits you on the right cheek, offer him your left cheek as well.' *(Matthew 5:21-22, 38-39)*

3. Outstanding examples from history and today

(a) St Wulfstan – getting laws changed for the better

Wulfstan was an English boy, born a long time ago in Saxon times. He went to abbey schools, in Evesham and in Peterborough. He became a monk at Worcester Abbey at the time the country and the Church were in trouble. Wulfstan was soon given an important position, as the prior of the abbey. He quietly made improvements, and his twelve monks began to see that it was a good thing to follow the rule of the monastery. After some years there were over 50 monks in the abbey. Wulfstan was then made bishop. He wasn't too happy about this because he preferred to work quietly in the monastery. But he was a brilliant leader; he listened to the people and worked very hard for them. He had only been the bishop for three years when the Normans invaded the country. That was in 1066.

Somehow, Bishop Wulfstan kept his diocese free from trouble as he helped everyone accept the new laws and way of life. He did have some problems with the barons, and with Welsh soldiers crossing the border. But Wulfstan was a humble, kind man, and he even managed to stop the slave trade in Bristol. He built new churches and persuaded the priests to obey church laws better. Because he gave a good example by following the Benedictine rule closely, people loved him. They knew he could have lived in style as a rich bishop. They looked at their leader and saw that obeying sensible rules was a good thing.

(b) William Wilberforce – getting slavery abolished, by law

Anglican churches celebrate the life of William Wilberforce on 30 July. They recognise him as a saintly person. He was born in Hull, in 1759. His father was a wealthy merchant and sent his son to Cambridge University. He was only 21 years old when he was made an MP (Member of Parliament) for Hull. A few years later, on a European tour, he became an enthusiastic Christian. He knew that he must work in Parliament to change unjust laws. He became a 'workaholic' MP! He never stopped, making speeches, investigating abuses and encouraging changes in the law. Meanwhile he was a keen Christian, a member of an Evangelical group, called the 'Clapham Sect'. They worked hard to improve the life of communities. They also supported missionaries and founded the Bible Society.

Of all the causes William Wilberforce worked for, he is remembered for his long struggle to persuade the government to get rid of slavery. (St Wulfstan had tried to do this 800 years earlier.) William succeeded in 1807, but slaves were still used in British Colonies, especially in the West Indian sugar plantations. He kept on and on arguing against the law that allowed slavery abroad. He lived just long enough to hear that Parliament had got rid of (abolished) slavery altogether. He died in the same year, 1833.

(c) King Alfred the Great – legal code based on common sense and Christian mercy

If you ask people what they know about King Alfred the Great, they are likely to say: 'Not a lot.' Some will tell you that he burnt the cakes! We don't know where that came from. What we do know is that he was a splendid king. He was king of the West Saxons in the ninth century. He was only 22 when he became king, and he very quickly stopped the threat of more Danes coming into Britain. He set about bringing peace to the land, and to the Church.

Alfred ruled by example. He gave half his money to start religious houses of monks and nuns. They became centres for teaching the children, looking after the sick and giving comfort to the poor and to travellers. He never missed his daily Mass, and translated many church writings into English. He revised the country's laws. He based them on ordinary common sense, so that people would understand. But he also made sure that they were inspired by the Gospel of compassion. Anglicans remember him on 26 October, the date of his death in 899.

(d) St Thomas More – upholding church law

Thomas More was a Londoner, born in the fifteenth century. He studied the law and became such a brilliant lawyer that the king, Henry VIII, noticed him. Seeing that he was an honest, clever and charming man, the king made him a Member of Parliament, as Chancellor of England. This was a very important job. He became Speaker of the House, and an ambassador for England. This made him a wealthy and popular man. He was also known for his happy family life and his love of the Catholic faith. Everything was going well for him, until Henry VIII had problems with the Catholic Church. The king was married but wanted to have a new wife. Thomas would not agree with this, so the angry king sent Thomas to prison. Thomas had to make a choice: to obey the wishes of the king, or to be loyal to the Church and accept her laws. Thomas refused to accept the new law of the king that would make him, Henry, the head of the Catholic Church in England. So Thomas was taken to Tower Hill and executed. Just before he died he said: 'I am the king's good servant, but God's first.'

(e) Pandita Mary Ramabai – a Hindu/Christian who fought for changes in the law

Ramabai was a Hindu, born in India in 1858. Her father was a learned Brahmin: that meant he was important and respected. He believed in educating girls, which was unusual. So Ramabai was taught to read, especially the Hindu Scriptures. In the course of a great famine, her parents and sister died. Her father's last words to her were: 'Remember, you are my youngest, most beloved child; I have given you into the hands of our God. You are his, and to him alone you must belong, and serve him all your life.'

This is exactly what she did. She and her brother were taken in by the Anglican missionaries in Calcutta. Later she became a Christian, taking the name Mary. But she always kept her Hindu spirit. Her life was quite a struggle, especially when her husband died soon after their daughter was born. She was a strong woman, and refused to accept laws that she saw as unjust. She was opposed to the Hindu caste system (it said that not all people were equal), and the tradition of child marriages.

Eventually, after studying and teaching in both England and America, she returned to India. There she set up schools for the poorest Indian girls, child widows and unwanted child wives and daughters. She spoke out boldly on their behalf. Meanwhile she translated the Bible into her own Indian language.

Mary Ramabai was an unusual Christian, because she refused to belong to any one group of Christians (Anglicans, Methodists, Baptists, etc.). She followed the Christian Gospel, but did not like all the rules that kept Christians apart.

Today, 80 years after her death, many Christians would agree with her free spirit. It was said of her that 'she wished to fly with the swallows and soar with the lark' in the open sky. Mary Ramabai was given the honorary title Pandita, in India; and Anglicans recognise her holiness and celebrate her life on 30 April.

4. Extra material

It may be useful to have a short discussion with the pupils about the *Commonwealth of Nations*. Perhaps show the children a passport and read out its title: European Community. United Kingdom of Great Britain and Northern Ireland. British citizen. This gives us our national identity.

British means to have: a common language, a common history, a common religion (which, by tradition, is Christianity).

However, many British people today speak Punjabi, Urdu, Chinese. Many children born here have parents or grandparents who were born in Africa, Asia, the Caribbean, China, Russia, etc. Many children may not be Christian, but Buddhist, Rastafarian, Hindu, Muslim or Sikh. We call this 'Multicultural Britain.'

This mixture of nations is nothing new. Britain had a Roman past, a Viking past, an Anglo-Saxon past, etc. (Refer to the children's history lessons.)

British Empire:

Empires are groups of countries under one rule. They are formed by invading armies and trade between lands. In the seventeenth century the British made some overseas settlements, called colonies. They went in search of gold, then tobacco. It was the time of the slave trade. Later merchants travelled to set up tea and coffee plantations. Britons emigrated (left Britain) and became wealthy landowners. The colonies grew and eventually became the British Empire. In the nineteenth century Queen Victoria was queen of a large Empire. But countries were not always happy to be under British rule. America had separated from Britain in the eighteenth century. By the twentieth century other countries wanted to be independent (manage their own affairs). By 1980 the Empire had disappeared.

Commonwealth of Nations:

In 1931 Parliament gave some British Empire countries (Canada, Australia and New Zealand) special status. They were not ruled by Britain any more, but kept a special link with us, especially for trade. The English-speaking countries were now called the British Commonwealth of Nations. Later on the word British was dropped. Today all the countries are loosely organised and the Queen is no longer seen as their Head of State. But all the 50 countries of the Commonwealth keep cultural and trading links. They make up one-quarter of the world's population. Some countries are rich, others are very poor.

The Commonwealth of Nations believe in:

- international peace;
- rule of international law;
- each individual equal under the law;
- equal rights for people of all races, whatever their gender, colour, creed or political belief;
- freedom from oppression for all human life;
- the right to decent living standards for all people, and opportunities to follow their aspirations.

5. Prayer and hymn

Our Father in heaven,
you yourself have taught us
that without some rules and regulations
life would soon become a chaos.
Give us the good sense to obey them
for the good of those we live with,
and the good sense to change them
as the world we live in changes.
But above all, help us to obey
the one law your Son Jesus taught us:
to love you, and because of that,
all the people you have given us
to live with. Amen.

Appropriate hymns:

  25 A new commandment I give unto you
122 How lovely on the mountains
145 I was so glad
188 Love is the only law

6. Suggestions for follow-up work

(a) Research the Commonwealth of Nations. Find out the 50 countries. Identify them on a large map. Find out about the Commonwealth Games. (If appropriate, use this event to introduce the topic.)

(b) Explore the idea that the Christian Churches are a kind of Commonwealth of Christian believers. Finally compare the six beliefs of the Commonwealth of Nations with the Gospel.

7. Vocabulary

Fairness, rights, responsibility, laws, discussion, debate, voting, Parliament.

9. Respect for property
Unit 9 of Citizenship syllabus

1. Suggestions from the syllabus

(a) Different kinds of responsibilities
(b) Rights and duties in the home
(c) Rights and duties in school and the community
(d) Right and wrong – stealing, shoplifting, vandalism
(e) Property – respect, caring, communal facilities
(f) Use of resources for the community

Introduction:

This unit can be focused on the whole school community. It is an opportunity to talk to the pupils about all the staff – the secretaries, the dinner staff, the librarians, the caretakers, the chaplain, etc., as well as the teachers and pupils. It would be useful to have ideas from all the staff about areas that need discussing with the pupils.

(a) Invite some of the above staff to the assembly. Each could then tell the children their responsibility; for example, 'My responsibility is to see that you get a proper meal to keep you healthy'; 'My responsibility is to keep the library in good order, so that you can easily find the book you need, and my responsibility is to keep it tidy, so that it is a nice environment for you to be in'; 'My responsibility is to keep the whole school safe for you. I need to make sure there are no dangerous, broken pieces of apparatus. And I have a responsibility to remove the rubbish, so that everywhere is clean for you'.

(b) Throw out a challenge to the children. Ask them to keep a diary for a week – in which they note down the duties that their parents or grandparents give them (e.g. tidying their bedroom; helping in the kitchen). What are the duties they have – without being reminded by their parents? (This is a difficult one and would need unravelling in class discussion: e.g. the duty to be considerate to their family members; the duty to be loyal; the duty to be helpful, etc.)

(c) Communities are groups of people who share something together. The first community we belong to is our family. School is an important community, because we share hours, days, weeks, months, years of our lives together. Our church is another special community. This is an opportunity to introduce St Paul's idea of the community – like a body. Using this model, you can show that if one part of the body is not working well, it upsets the whole body. Bring some children onto the platform in bandages and with crutches. The girl with the 'broken' arm says that she cannot do the washing-up for a month. The boy with the crutches says that he cannot go to the shops for his mum, etc. A girl with no handicap says, 'Oh no! that means I've got to do all the jobs.' Point out that this could lead to arguing and that makes the whole family fed up, and cross. On the other hand, it could lead to the whole family helping one another generously. The boy with crutches says that at least he can stand by the sink and do the washing-up. The girl with the broken arm says that she can read to her little sister, etc.

(d) Right and wrong in the community.

A community is happy when its members are thoughtful and generous towards each other. If the members are selfish and only think of them-selves the community can become very unhappy. A community works when each member obeys the rules set up for that community. (Which is not to say that all rules are permanent and never need to be modified.) Some rules *every* community needs to obey. Remind the children of the Ten Commandments. Highlight the commandment 'Thou shalt not steal'. Explore with the children the consequences for the community when people steal or shoplift. Show how vandalism is a form of stealing. It deprives the community of a good environment – which is their right, etc.

(e) Respect for communal property could then be discussed. Your school may have a litter problem, or disorder in the changing rooms, etc. Pro-duce an 'Ideas Box' and invite the children to suggest the ways they could improve care for school facilities. Perhaps make it an inter-class competition, to come up with the best ideas.

(f) On a wider issue: it may be possible to encourage your pupils to consider the needs of some disadvantaged members of your local community. Perhaps, for example, a playgroup is in need of toys to replace broken ones. Some of the children might like to make posters for a 'toys appeal', and your school could organise the collection.

The needs of your local community will inspire other suggestions.

2. Sacred writings: readings and reflections

It may be an appropriate time to consider the 'community' sacraments of Communion and Reconciliation whilst working around this Unit: (i) Holy Communion as the presence of Jesus to unite his followers as a community; (ii) The need for forgiveness when we hurt the community.

(a) The Ten Commandments

Retell the Ten Commandments story from Unit 2 and then highlight:

(i) The sixth Commandment:
Love your neighbour by never doing them any harm (stealing).

(ii) The eighth Commandment:
Love your neighbour by respecting their things.

(b) Forgiveness of those who do wrong

(i) O Lord, there is no other God like you,
always forgiving, always calming your anger,
always showing unchanging love,
always taking away our sins,
and sending them to the bottom of the sea,
always true to your people,
as you lovingly promised long ago. *(From Micah 7:18-19)*

(ii) The prayer that Jesus taught us –

God of all people in the world,
close to us as a father or mother,
yet far beyond us as the sky,
we fall on our knees in wonder before you.

We long for your Kingdom
when all people will live in your way,
and the world will be a heaven on earth.

Unless you give us food every day, we will die:
teach us to share it fairly.
Unless you forgive us every day, we will be without hope:
teach us to forgive others the way you do.

If you put us to the test,
you know how easily we could let you down.
Rescue us therefore
as you have always rescued your people.

For you are the God we will always turn to
in sorrow and in joy.
We mean this. *(From Matthew 6:9-13)*

(iii) Peter came to Jesus and asked, 'If my brother keeps on sinning against me, how many times do I have to forgive him? As many as seven times?' 'No, not seven times,' answered Jesus, 'but seventy times seven, that's to say, endlessly.' *(From Matthew 18:21-22)*

That's what the Kingdom of God is all about.

(iv) When Jesus was dying on the cross, he said: 'Father, forgive them! They don't know what they are doing.' *(From Luke 23:34)*

(c) The Body of Christ

St Paul described the community of the Church as the Body of Christ:

> All of you together make up the Body of Christ.
> Each one of you is a part of it.
> God himself has arranged bodies in such a way
> as to give the greatest dignity to the parts that need it most.
> In this way, there is total agreement:
> every part of the body is concerned for every other part.
> When one part is hurt, every other part hurts with it;
> when one part gets on well, they're all happy.
>
> *(1 Corinthians 12:27, 24-26)*

3. Outstanding examples from history and today

Here are some examples of individuals showing outstanding respect for others, especially for those usually excluded from community who are often regarded as no more than 'property'.

(a) Elizabeth Fry – respect for the poor, including prisoners

In every community some are richer, and some poorer than others. Today, even the poorest people in our country can go to school, visit the doctor and have somewhere to live. It is hard to imagine, but there was a time in England when the poor missed out. Some women had to steal to feed their children, and they were then sent to harsh prisons. The children went with them. Some mothers were put on 'convict ships' and sent to colonies like Australia. The poor were treated like useless property, and thrown away.

They found a saviour in Elizabeth Fry. She was the wife of a banker and they had eleven children. The Fry family were Quakers, Christians who were known for their generosity. Elizabeth visited the women and children in Newgate Prison, London. She was appalled at the filthy conditions they lived in. She spent the rest of her life working to improve conditions in the prisons and on the 'convict ships'. She made the authorities respect the women by giving them their own prison, with women staff. She started a school for the children, and sewing classes for their mothers. Later, she worked to prevent the women going to prison, by setting up night shelters for the homeless. She was also the first person to set up training for nurses. It is amazing that this kind lady, who had such a large family, found time to do all this. They say that she never neglected her own children, but taught them to care for the poor too. She is remembered on 12 October, the day she died in 1845.

(b) Caroline Chisholm – worked for abused women who were regarded as 'property'

Caroline was only a little girl when Elizabeth Fry was busy in her reform work in prisons and convict ships. When Caroline grew up, she married a Roman Catholic army officer. She became a Catholic like him. They moved to Madras in India, where she founded a school for soldiers' daughters, because they were treated badly.

In 1838 they went on holiday leave to Australia, and were shocked to see the state of the poor women still arriving from England. Many of them were the wives of convicts who had been sent out to New South Wales. Unfortunately, the hostel that had been set up by Elizabeth Fry was now standing empty, and was full of rats. The authorities were doing nothing to help the women.

Caroline was angry that women were shown no respect and were treated almost as slaves. She stayed on in Australia with her two small children. (Her husband joined her as soon as he could.) The family began a long campaign to change the laws on immigration. Caroline persuaded the British government to help the immigrants especially by improving the ships. She managed to get the Australian government to help them by providing decent hostels. But not before she had settled thousands of immigrants herself, and reunited 600 families. The Chisholms returned to England for a short while and, with help from Lord Shaftesbury, they persuaded the British government to change the emigration laws. Charles Dickens wrote about the lives of the wives and children of convicts, in order to help them.

Caroline and her family spent over 20 years in Australia, and they were able to change the lives of thousands of people, bringing to an end the disgraceful treatment of poor women and children. Caroline had been supported in her work by the Anglican Church, and it is this Church that remembers her on 16 May, for her outstanding Christian service of the poor.

(c) Sister Helen Prejean – respect for life, including death-cell prisoners

Sister Helen is a Roman Catholic nun who lives in America. She is rather like Elizabeth Fry, because she has spent her own life trying to make life more bearable for prisoners. She has become well known today because a film was made about her and shown across the world. It was called *Dead Man Walking*.

In some countries people who commit murder are sentenced to death, as in some American States today. We used to do this in England, but the law was changed, and our prisoners are simply imprisoned for a very long time. Sister Helen visits the prisoners who are going to be put to death (executed). Like most Christians, she does not believe it is right to kill the prisoners. She believes that we should respect the lives of sinners, even the worst criminals. Jesus said that everyone is forgiven by God, and that people should act the same way.

Sister Helen has a hard time. People would far sooner 'get rid' of the criminals she visits. She said: 'Once I used to just ask God (in the Bidding Prayers at Mass) to comfort people suffering, like the prisoners. Then I realised that I had to be the one to do the comforting, for him!'

(d) Octavia Hill – respect for property and housing the homeless

One of the rights that every person has is the right to have a home to live in. It is the responsibility of the government to provide enough houses for everyone. This is not easy. Today, our government does reasonably well, but it was not always so. In the nineteenth century, during Victorian times, the cities were overcrowded and families often lived in slums. Some were homeless. One woman who was determined to do something about it was a teacher, called Octavia Hill. She was horrified by the poor homes her pupils lived in. So with the help of the artist John Ruskin she borrowed money, and bought three slum dwellings in London. She believed that if she taught the families to respect and look after the property they would become happier in their poor environment.

Octavia was the first person to introduce the rights and duties of landlord and tenant (a landlord owns the property, a tenant pays to live there). She often sat down with families who had little money, and showed them how to use it wisely. From this her work grew. She took over more properties, including some that were owned by the Church. She set up training centres in housing management in other English cities, and then her work spread to Germany, Holland and the United States. Octavia knew that when people have a good environment to live in, their lives become richer. So she also advised the government to open up the private London squares to *all* the people, and recommended that open spaces were left in towns for people's recreation.

Octavia was inspired to work hard for the poor because she quietly followed the Gospel. She was a humble lady and absolutely refused the suggestion that she deserved to be buried in Westminster Abbey. But the Anglican Church still remembers her, and honours her on 13 August, the day she died in 1912.

4. Extra material

As this unit is very much about local communities, it would be appropriate for you to collect material from the local newspaper. Build up a noticeboard about projects to improve the community.

5. Prayer and hymn

Our Father in heaven,
be a father to us on earth.
Teach us to respect all your children
as our brothers and sisters,
with whom we are happy to share our things
but never to presume to take what is theirs.
We ask this in the name of Jesus your Son,
who shared with us all he had and all he was. Amen.

Appropriate hymns:

131 I give my hands to do your work
208 O Lord, all the world belongs to you
220 Our Father
299 We are one family together

6. Suggestions for follow-up work

(a) Draw the outline of a body. The children draw their own face, and each one is stuck inside the shape. Fill the complete space by adding other faces, representing the whole school community.

(b) It is possible that a parent or friend of the school works in the local community. If it is appropriate, engage some of your pupils in helping to improve the environment. For example, creating a frieze to decorate a bare wall in a residential home; painting over a graffitied wall at the youth club; tidying up the church garden.

7. Vocabulary

Right and wrong, stealing, shoplifting, punishment, vandalism, victim, offender, prison, consequences, respect, sharing, belongings, buildings, law, community facilities.

10. Local democracy for young citizens

Unit 10 of Citizenship syllabus

1. Suggestions from the syllabus

(a) Local community, local council
(b) Roles of the leaders and councillors, the mayor
(c) Spiritual, moral, social and cultural issues – understanding how others experience these
(d) Voting, debating, elections – responsibility

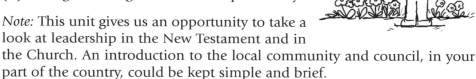

Note: This unit gives us an opportunity to take a look at leadership in the New Testament and in the Church. An introduction to the local community and council, in your part of the country, could be kept simple and brief.

(a) Describe the town hall (or equivalent) to your pupils. See if they recognise the building you describe. You could have a kind of guessing game with them, and describe other local buildings first, and let them tell you what you are describing.

   When they have guessed the 'town hall', ask them what goes on there. Who works there? The answer you want is: the local council, led by councillors, the mayor, and perhaps a sheriff.

(b) It is difficult to see how young children would be very interested in the work of local councillors. They may be more interested in the mayor, who dresses up in hat, gown and chain. Ideally, the class could visit the town hall and council chamber; and meet the mayor. Failing this, you could role play a meeting, with the discussion being on a hypothetical issue the pupils would relate to, for example, spending money either on improving school playgrounds (for safety reasons), or on providing your school with a larger staffroom.

(c) The syllabus asks you in this unit to consider the multicultural and multifaith experience within your local community. This could be an opportunity to make, with the pupils, a survey of the different groups local to your school. Have a very large, simplified map of your town, or region, placed in the corridor. Locate the churches of different denominations: synagogue, mosque, etc. Locate restaurants: Chinese, Indian, Thai, French, Italian, etc. Inner-city schools will have more examples to explore. If your local professional football team has some 'overseas' players, or your hospital has recruited nurses from abroad, why not invite some of these to an assembly? Ask them to tell the children what it 'feels' like to be away from their own countries, families and familiar way of life. What has made them feel welcome? What has not?

(d) Elections: the responsibility of debating and voting. Abstract talk about this would be totally inappropriate for young children. At the time of local or national elections, hold simple elections in your classes. Let each class vote for a 'leader' for a role you can create for your class. Use a simple method that introduces some of the democratic process we follow in elections: candidates, their teams of supporters, their 'manifesto', election posters, etc. If appropriate in your school, introduce candidates to the assembly; or announce the results of form 'elections' at the school assembly.

2. Sacred writings: readings and reflections

This unit is about the role of leadership in the community, as well as about working together as a community. It is also about the different tasks that members of the group are given. This can relate to the calling of the apostles by Jesus, and their community organisation after his death and resurrection. It may be an opportunity to recall the great leaders of the Jewish people too.

(a) The story of Abraham

Abraham is the father of the Jewish people. He was chosen by God to be the leader of a new nation. He lived a very long time ago (about 1800 BC). We can read his story in the first book of the Bible, called Genesis. The story tells us that God asked him to leave everything behind and set out for an unknown land, where he would learn about God and become the father of a new race which was to be the special 'People of God'. Abraham's life was full of difficulties, but he never lost his faith (that is, his *belief* that God was guiding him and would look after him).

(b) The story of Moses

> Since then, there has never been such a prophet like Moses, the man who knew God face to face, like a friend. *(Deuteronomy 34:10)*

The Old Testament (the Jewish sacred writings) is full of admiration for Moses. He was the man who led the Jewish people through the desert, out of Egypt, where they had been prisoners. He is the leader who organised the way the community should live. He had an agreement with God, a covenant, about how people should behave. He gave them the Ten Commandments. He is the great law-giver. (See also Unit 2.)

(c) The story of Jesus

Of course, for Christians, the great leader is Jesus. Show the children how Jesus led first and foremost by his example. He was humble, brave, full of compassion and forgiving. Ask the children to give examples of this. Jesus was a carpenter/builder, but he became the leader of a small group of friends – the apostles. He left his first job to become a teacher who shared his ideas about God, his Father, with the crowds who came to listen to him. The first followers of Jesus (who were Jews, like Jesus) called him a new Moses.

The early Christian writer to the Hebrews wrote:

> Never take your eyes off Jesus,
> a leader who shared our weakness with us
> and was tempted in all ways we are tempted . . .
> Like us he could only learn to be close to God
> through suffering . . .
> Never lose sight of Jesus,
> who leads us on our journey to God. *(Hebrews 5:1-8; 12:2)*

(d) The story of Peter and the early Church

When Jesus died, the apostles who were his friends were at first lost. They met together in an upstairs room, and a strange thing happened. They were sad and frightened when they entered the room, but they changed dramatically. They were suddenly filled with courage and determination to carry on Jesus' teaching. They were filled with Jesus' spirit – we call this the Holy Spirit. They left the room as changed people. They organised themselves, with leaders and helpers, to spread the Good News they had heard from Jesus. Peter took over as leader. Jesus had promised that this would happen (he had called him 'the Rock', on which the future Church would be built). We can read about the way these first Christians (as the followers of Jesus Christ were now being called) organised themselves and elected new leaders and helpers in the Acts of the Apostles (the choice of Matthias in Chapter 1, and the choice of Stephen and six others in Chapter 6).

3. Outstanding examples from history and today

(a) St Peter – the unlikely leader

His name wasn't always Peter. His parents called him Simon, and he had a brother called Andrew. They grew up to be fishermen. Perhaps Jesus knew them because he mended their boats. Jesus noticed them when he wanted some friends to help him preach about the Kingdom of God. Simon was strong and enthusiastic. He was always first to jump in with an opinion. In fact, he sometimes spoke without thinking and people called him a 'hot-head'. But Jesus liked Simon's enthusiasm, and he changed his name to

Peter, which means 'rock'. He knew that one day Peter would be strong enough, like a firm rock, to be the foundation of the first church communities.

After the Resurrection it was Peter who took charge of things. He became really brave and travelled as a preacher, carrying on Jesus' work. He went as far as Rome, and there he was put to death, like Jesus, on a cross. (People didn't like this new religion.) Peter is buried in Rome and Roman Catholics think of him as their first pope, or leader. That is why popes live in Rome. Peter is good news for all leaders. Leaders don't have to be perfect; Peter certainly wasn't. He made many mistakes, especially when he ran away scared, after Jesus died.

St Peter's feast day is on 29 June.

(b) St Paul – the missionary leader, and co-founder of the early Church

Peter did not found the early Christian Church on his own. Paul was a very important organiser, in the years following Jesus' death. Like Peter, Paul was enthusiastic. But his first enthusiasm was to get rid of the Christians. He felt that they were criticising his Jewish faith. He was riding to Damascus one day, determined to stop the Christians from preaching, when he heard Jesus 'speak' to him – in his head, and heart. Paul was so shocked (believing as he did that Jesus had died) that he fell off his horse. He changed completely and began to preach as a follower of Jesus. Everyone was amazed.

Paul was a bundle of energy. He travelled thousands of miles, setting up Christian communities that he called 'churches'. He wrote to all his churches, teaching them how to become good followers of Jesus. He usually wrote kind words, but sometimes he was angry when the people behaved badly. He had exciting adventures, getting shipwrecked and taken prisoner. His life was hard, and in the end he was executed. But Christians will never forget Paul, who like a human tornado caused an uproar wherever he went. He made people sit up and listen – and organise themselves into communities that followed Jesus. He was a very good leader.

St Paul's feast day is celebrated on 29 June, with St Peter.

(c) Saints Adrian and Theodore (seventh century) – they worked together as a team

It is really most important for leaders of a community to work together as a team. In the seventh century the Church in England was having a difficult time. The land was ruled by the Saxons, who had not been Christians for very long. The different 'kingdoms' in England were still at war with each other, and the Church was finding it hard to work alongside the kings. To add to the problems, a terrible plague had killed some of the bishops (leaders of the Christian communities).

The Pope decided to sort things out. He asked an African monk, who was living in Italy, to go to England as their Archbishop of Canterbury – the top job. But the monk, called Adrian, told the Pope that there was someone who could do a better job. This was Theodore, an elderly Greek monk, who lived in Rome.

So the Pope sent both of them to England. Theodore went as the new Archbishop of Canterbury, and Adrian took charge of the monastery and the school at Canterbury. They became a perfect team. Theodore travelled all over England and worked out a way of organising the Church better. He divided the country up into areas, called dioceses. Each one was given a bishop. Meanwhile Adrian began to train young men to be priests because he knew Theodore needed them in the parishes. A parish was a small area looked after by a priest. This is the way the Church is organised today.

In 672, only three years after he arrived, Theodore was able to hold the first big meeting of all the bishops in England. It was held in Hertford. By the time of the next big church meeting in Hatfield, seven years later, Archbishop Theodore had managed to organise the whole country into a united and well-run Church. He did this in spite of the English kingdoms being constantly at war.

The Church today is organised in the way Theodore invented: dioceses and parishes. Our parish is . . . . in the diocese of . . . .

(d) Mary Slessor, born 1848 – missionary who became a magistrate

Mary came from a very poor Presbyterian Christian family in Scotland. At 11 years old she went to work in the mill. She loved going to church because she heard wonderful stories about the brave missionaries who worked in Africa amongst some very dangerous people. The Calabar people in Nigeria were the most dangerous, because the white people had gone there to buy them as slaves. They used gin and rum to pay for them, which didn't help the Calabar people at all. Eventually, Mary achieved her ambition to become a missionary amongst these people: she had joined an evening class to prepare herself. She was very small, only five foot tall, and everyone said she was silly to go out to that part of Africa.

But Mary was amazing. She was very strong-willed and determined. She quickly learnt the *Efik* language and began to visit the tribal chiefs. She talked to them easily and persuaded them to listen to her ideas about God and about how to behave. She was sent to work among a fierce tribe, called the *Okoyong*. They had some hideous practices, like sacrificing human beings, and killing the second-born of twins. Mary was determined to save these lives. So she started an orphanage for twins, and stood up to the tribal chiefs, with great courage. (She hit one over the head with her umbrella!) The people found her just and sensible, and everyone grew to love her. The British government heard about her, and made her the official British representative to the *Okoyong* people. Mary organised their trade and became their magistrate. She settled their problems and arguments. Even the tribal chiefs accepted her and changed their bad laws. She died in Nigeria and was buried with her beloved *Okoyong* tribe. They called her *Eka kpukru owo*, which means 'everyone's mother'.

The Anglican Church celebrates her life on 11 January, the day she died in 1915.

(e) Samuel and Henrietta Barnett – a husband and wife who were very good at getting things done for the poor

Samuel Barnett was the vicar of the Victorian slum parish of St Jude's in Whitechapel. He and his wife, Henrietta, worked there for over 40 years, and found ways to improve the lives of their people. They set up, with others, the Charity Organisation Society. They were friends of Octavia Hill (see Unit 9), who was organising better housing for the poor. Together they worked out ways of encouraging people to improve their lives. In those Victorian days there were no such things as city councils to work out ways to make life good for everyone. It was usually Christian people who found ways to help others.

Samuel was always worried about the enormous gap between the rich people and the poor. The poor had no way they could really enjoy life. So with Henrietta he set up entertainment evenings in their parish. Then they started reading classes, discussion groups and art classes. Samuel started the Whitechapel Art Gallery for their work. He also wanted everyone to have the chance to go to university, just as he had done. He hated the way the poor were treated as 'second best'. Today the local council tries to make sure that all people have equal opportunities in education, housing and jobs. The government in Victorian England recognised what Samuel was doing and made him their Poor Law Guardian.

Henrietta lived for many years after Samuel died, and became the first woman Poor Law Guardian. She founded a charity fund that gave slum children holidays in the countryside. Her main work was to help in founding a new type of community in London. It is called Hampstead Garden Suburb. It was the first time all classes of people, rich and poor, were given the chance to live alongside each other. And she founded schools to educate girls from all the families. Henrietta Barnett School still exists today.

Samuel and Henrietta are a wonderful example of a couple who could have lived easy, comfortable lives. Instead, they chose to spend their time helping other people to live comfortable community lives. The Anglican Church remembers them on 17 June.

4. Extra material

Organisation in the Church

This is an opportunity to give the children a vocabulary related to the organisation of your Church. For example, Catholic schools could give the following words:

Archbishop: leader of a province of the Church.

Bishop: leader of a diocese (which is smaller than a province).

Bishops' Conference: a meeting of bishops to make decisions about the Church in their own country.

Cardinal: a close adviser to the Pope.

Church: the followers of Jesus; and the building where they meet.

Deacon: a man chosen to help the priest in a large parish. He can be a married man.

Diocese: a group of parishes, led by the bishop.

Diocesan Pastoral Council: members of the people and priests, elected from different parishes, to advise the bishop.

General Council: a meeting of all the bishops in Rome when important decisions are needed. They are not held very often.

Laity: the people who belong to the Church, but are not ordained ministers.

Parish: the community of Catholics in a small area.

Parish Council: a group of laity who have been elected to organise the running of the parish with priest/s.

Pope: the leader of the Catholic Church.

Priest: the leader of the parish community, who helps the bishop.

Province: a large area into which a country is divided, to make Church organisation easier.

Synod: a meeting of all the bishops in Rome, held every two years.

Vatican: the part of Rome where St Peter is buried and the headquarters of the Catholic Church.

5. Prayer and hymn

> Our Leader in heaven,
> look down on your people and see
> how much we need good leaders on earth,
> locally and regionally, nationally and worldwide.
> Give us the generosity to support them
> in the difficult task we ask them to do,
> and the good sense to change them

when that becomes necessary.
We make this prayer in the name of Jesus
who continues to lead us to you. Amen.

Appropriate hymns:

216 On our school your blessing, Lord
257 Take my hands
272 There are people who live in mansions
280 A voice from the bush said: Moses

6. Suggestions for follow-up work

(a) Being a leader is not easy. Leaders have to overcome problems. You could illustrate this with the story of Moses and the ten plagues. It offers the children a colourful, artistic opportunity to make a classroom frieze.

(b) Invite the school chaplain or a local priest or, preferably, the bishop to an assembly to explain how the parish and diocese work. It would be best if he is supported by some of the lay parish/diocesan council members, for example, the secretary or the head of a commission or two . . . Produce for the school noticeboard a plan of the diocese and its churches and schools.

(c) Expand on the above activity by making a display of the whole Church organisation – using the vocabulary on page 85.

7. Vocabulary

Place, location, map, feature, councils, councillors, mayor, Members of Parliament, voting, debate, elections.

11. In the media – what's in the news?

Unit 11 of Citizenship syllabus

1. Suggestions from the syllabus

(a) Important role of the media – communicating local, national and international news

(b) Communication

(c) Social issues treated in the soaps

(d) Values and attitudes shown

(e) Creating news sheets

(f) Danger of bias. Influences for good and bad

Introduction

This unit of the Citizenship syllabus is an enormous challenge. It seems sophisticated material for this age group. However, it would be possible to introduce young children to the idea of distributing news through the written word, cinema, television and the Internet. After all, many children use computers and even have a television in their bedroom. The assembly material could take some preparation.

(a) Call some children up to the platform to mime watching, listening, reading etc. Show them a card for their activity. The others have to guess what they are doing: watching television, reading a paper, listening to the radio.

(b) Take one piece of topical news and quite simply show the children how it is reported in the media. Select an item that is not too heavy, for example, an outstanding sports result like England winning a gold medal. Read a newspaper report of the event. Show it on a video. Print out an Internet report. Speak to someone on your mobile about it: 'Have you heard the news . . .?'

Point out that news can travel fast and that news can be reported from different viewpoints.

(c) Before you start this unit it would be a good idea to find out from your pupils which programmes they watch, especially the soaps. What are their favourite children's programmes? If appropriate, select a favourite programme that offers you the opportunity to discuss social issues and values suggested by the programme.

(d) Show a dramatic piece of video at the assembly. For example, the great whale's tail emerging from the water in the David Attenborough programme. Discuss the effect it has on you. 'Wow! Amazing! Powerful! What photography! . . .'

Follow this by a reading from Psalm 104.

(e) Creating news sheets. This is a classroom activity, but it could be introduced at the assembly. When you have an interesting school event – sports day or an outing to a local museum – follow it up with a report back at the next assembly. Put out the challenge to create a newspaper page about the event. Make it a competition, with the results to go on show, and the year group or staff to choose the winners.

(f) The danger of bias. Make up some newspaper headlines, in pairs. Two headlines describing the same event, but from different viewpoints.

1. Event: Liverpool 2, Leeds 1

   THE REDS ARE BEST AGAIN (*Liverpool Echo*)
   BEST TEAM LOSES AGAIN (*Leeds Post*)

2. Event: A General Election

   DISASTROUS DAY FOR LABOUR (*The Mirror*)
   CELEBRATIONS AS TORIES TRIUMPH (*The Sun*)

2. Sacred writings: readings and reflections

This is the opportunity to talk a little about the Gospels as the 'Good News'. There were no televisions, videos or films 2000 years ago. We can only know about Jesus through the written word. People write in different ways. We've probably discovered that already in Literacy Hour. The first words written down about Jesus were in letters (epistles) that Paul sent to the churches. Then the four Gospels were written: Mark (about AD 65), Matthew (about AD 75), Luke (about AD 85), John (about AD 95).

It is important to know that the Gospels are not biographies. The writers used facts and stories about Jesus to show that they believed he was the Son of God. The four writers were very different, and each used examples and facts about Jesus' life that attracted them most. For example, Luke was a doctor. He reports many of the healing miracles and the stories that showed how compassionate Jesus was. Luke probably became a doctor because he was a compassionate man himself.

(a) Isaiah already proclaims the Good News

What a thrill when a messenger
comes running down from the hills
with the good news of victory!
'Peace at last,' he announces in Jerusalem,
'our God rules over all!'
The city guards shout out for joy! (*Isaiah 52:7-8*)

(b) Jesus proclaims the Good News he has brought

God's Spirit is in my heart,
he has called me, and set me apart
to bring this Good News to the poor:
that prisoners will be prisoners no more,
that blind people will see,
that the downtrodden will be set free
and that the Good News for everyone
is that the Kingdom of God has come. *(Luke 4:18-19 [from Isaiah 61:1-2]*

(c) The Apostles are filled with the Spirit of Jesus, and go out to preach the Good News

On Pentecost Sunday, all the friends of Jesus held a meeting in a large room. Suddenly it sounded as if a storm had hit the house where they were meeting, and tongues of fire seemed to land on the heads of everyone in the room. It was the Spirit of Jesus, come to give them the courage to preach the Gospel. *(Acts 2:1-4)*

3. Outstanding examples from history and today

(a) Saints Perpetua and Felicity – they refused to say what was not true

One thing we often say, when we read a newspaper or magazine story, is, 'Is it true?'

Telling the truth is often quite difficult. Even our journalists (writers in the media) find it difficult. In order to sell newspapers you need exciting or shocking headlines. Sometimes journalists leave out parts of an event or make it sound more shocking than it really was, just to make sure they get the headlines. But even people who are not out to shock others can easily tell a lie to get out of trouble.

Many years ago there were two brave women who refused to tell even a small lie to get out of trouble. They knew that if they told the truth they would be put to death. But they still told the truth.

Perpetua was a Christian mother from north Africa. She had a friend, who was a slave. Her name was Felicity. They lived in the Roman Empire. The Emperor did not like the Christians and demanded that they should treat him as a god. Perpetua and Felicity refused to do so because they knew he was only a man. Perpetua was a noble lady and her family tried to make her tell a lie that would save her life. But she refused. We know all this because she kept a diary of the events that led to her capture and imprisonment, together with Felicity and four men. They were badly treated and finally taken to the arena to face wild animals. They died in AD 203, for telling the truth that they were followers of Jesus, the Son of God. We call them martyrs. We know how they died because other Christians hid Perpetua's diary, and completed the story of their martyrdom.

(b) St Bede – the writer, librarian, reporter

Did you know that the first libraries were set up by monks? One monk who spent hours in his library studying and writing was called Bede. He was a Geordie, born in Jarrow. He went to the monastery school at the age of 7 and stayed on to become a deacon, then a priest. He scarcely ever left the monastery, so his life was rather uneventful. But Bede was to be remembered across Europe for his remarkable skill in teaching and writing. He spent hours in the library, studying subjects in detail so that he could write well on many topics. You have the feeling that if Bede lived today, he could be a very good producer of documentary programmes. (A documentary is a film about a real issue, that has been studied seriously and presented fairly.)

Bede was very interested in Scripture, science and history. He wrote about the Bible, putting together earlier commentaries and adding his own thoughts. His scientific writings dealt with ways of calculating the calendar, and recording the traditional explanations for events like storms, famines and earthquakes. But Bede is mostly known for writing a history of the Church; he was very careful to use good sources. He was, therefore, an honest man of the media. You could probably see his history book in the adult section of your public library. It is one of the best records of life in Saxon times. Bede is known as St Bede the Venerable. 'Venerable' means 'worthy of respect'. We respect St Bede because he shows that the most ordinary job is worth doing well. He was an honest and careful writer, who always wanted to write what was true.

(c) Edith Cavell – she protected those who worked with her and saved their lives: a time to speak and a time to refuse to speak

Some of the stories reported in the media cause great pain to innocent people. Sometimes, to get an exciting story – to sell the paper, or win television viewers – editors tell stories about people's private lives. Many people believe that it is wrong to upset other people's lives.

Edith Cavell is honoured because she was a heroic victim of the First World War, refusing to speak out and get her nursing companions into trouble. Edith was the daughter of the Anglican vicar of Swardeston in Norfolk. As a young woman she travelled to Europe and visited a hospital in Bavaria. This gave her the idea to become a nurse. She returned home and worked in the Poor Law hospitals in London. After a few years Edith returned to Belgium to set up a Medical Institute to train nurses. She became the matron, the nurse in charge.

Seven years later, in 1914, the German army invaded Belgium and Edith stayed there to run the Red Cross hospital. The hospital nursed wounded soldiers from both sides: French, Belgian, English and German. The German authorities arrested Edith in 1915, accusing her of smuggling British soldiers out of Belgium into Holland.

Protecting those who worked with her, she was sentenced to death and executed by the firing squad on 12 October. As she calmly went to her death, Edith forgave her executioners, just as Jesus had done.

(d) St Maximilian Kolbe – newspaper editor

Maximilian Kolbe is a Polish saint who was put to death in a prison camp during the Second World War. He became a Franciscan priest, and was a brilliant scholar. Like many Polish Catholics, Maximilian had a great love for Jesus' mother, Mary. He wanted everyone to know the Good News of the Gospel and thought he could do this best through the media. He set up Catholic magazines and a newspaper, placing his work under the guidance of Mary. They were so successful that they had to add buildings to his monastery to house his newspaper press. Hundreds of young men joined him in his work.

As the war with Germany approached, Maximilian assured his readers that Jesus and his mother understood their suffering. When Germany invaded Poland all the Catholic newspapers were banned. When Maximilian refused to stop publishing he was arrested and sent to the Auschwitz prison camp. He was treated badly, but he amazed everyone by his kindness to other prisoners, even sharing his food with them. When a married man was sent to the punishment block, he volunteered to take his place. He quietly prayed and sang hymns until he was put to death. His feast day is kept on 14 August.

4. Extra material

(a) This is an appropriate time to look at the means of communication that have been developed over the ages: smoke signals; beacons; horseback; semaphore; Morse code; radio; telephone; television; computers; mobile phones . . .

(b) This is also an appropriate time to introduce the pupils to St Paul, as the great letterwriter. Paul wrote to the Christian communities (he called them 'churches') after he had visited them on his journeys. He was writing his letters (epistles) before the four Gospels were written.

5. Prayer and hymn

Our Father in heaven,
throughout the ages
there have been men and women

who have spread the Good News
of the Gospel,
even when it meant suffering.
Thank you for their courage.
Help us to put aside our fears
so that we can be bold in joining
your Son Jesus
to tell the world how much you love us. Amen.

Appropriate hymns:

  12 We will hear your Word
  97 God's Spirit is in my heart
223 Out to the great wide world we go

6. Suggestions for follow-up work

(a) Find an opportunity in the classroom for the pupils to work together
on a 'newspaper' or a pamphlet. Emphasise the need for good, honest
research to get the stories correct.

(b) A class activity could be to research the history of communication and
compile a large scrapbook to go into the school library.

(c) Invite a local newspaper reporter to your class to talk about their work,
and follow up with the children writing simple 'articles' or 'reports' on
a television programme, a film, or a sporting event, etc.

(d) Using resource books create a newspaper that is dated AD 33, with headlines that report the crucifixion. For older pupils it could be possible to
make two papers, one from the viewpoint of the disciples of Jesus and
one from the viewpoint of the Roman government.

7. Vocabulary

News story, article, feature, report, bias, balance, influence, information,
television, radio, cinema, newspaper, magazine, popular music, Internet.

Appendix

Useful Addresses

British Red Cross
9 Grosvenor Crescent, London SW1X 7EJ
Tel: 020 7201 5027
www.redcross,org.uk

British Trust for Conservation Volunteers
36 St Mary's Street, Wallingford
Oxford OX10 0EU

Cafod
Romero Close, Stockwell Road
London SW9 9TY Tel: 020 7733 7900
www.cafod.org.uk

Childline
2nd Floor, Royal Mail Building, Studd Street
London N1 0QW
Tel: 0171 239 1000
Helpline: 0800 1111

Christian Aid
35 Lower Marsh, Waterloo, London SE1 7RT
Tel: 020 7620 4444
www.christian-aid.org.uk

Civic Trust
17 Carlton House Terrace, London SW1Y 5AW

Commonwealth Institute
230 Kensington High Street, London W8 6NQ
Tel: 020 7603 45535
www.commonwealth.org.uk

Friends of the Earth
26-28 Underwood Street, London N1 7JQ
Tel: 020 7490 1555

Greenpeace
Canonbury Villas, London N1 2PN
Tel: 020 7865 8100

Habitat
(United Nations Centre for Human Settlements)
Europe Office Room E-6.1, Palais des Nations
1211 Geneva 10, Switzerland

Help the Aged
Unit 7, Kirkstall Industrial Park, Leeds LS4 2AZ

Lifeboats
Storm Force HQ, RNLI, West Quay Road, Poole
Dorset BH15 1HZ
www.rnli.org.uk

Medecins Sans Frontieres
124-132 Clerkenwell Road, London EC1R 5DL
www.msf.org

National Trust
36 Queen Anne's Gate, London SW1H 9AS

Oxfam
274 Banbury Road, Oxford OX2 7OZ
Tel: 01865 311 311
www.oxfaminternational.org

PDSA
Whitechapel Way, Priorslee, Telford, Shropshire
Tel: 01952 290 999

RSPB
The Lodge, Sandy, Beds SG19 2DL
Tel: 01767 680 551
www.rspb.org.uk

RSPCA
Causeway, Horsham, West Sussex RH12 1ZA
www.rspca.org.uk

Salvation Army
101 Newington Causeway, London SE1 6BN
Tel: 020 7367 4500
www.salvationarmy.org.uk

Save the Children
17 Grove Road, London SE5 8RD
Tel: 020 7703 5400
www.oneworld.org/scf/

Shelter
88 Old Street, London EC1V 9HU
Tel: 020 7505 2000
www.shelter.org.uk

Tear Fund
100 Church Road, Teddington TW11 8QE
Tel: 020 8977 9144

UNICEF
Africa House, 64-78 Kingsway, London WC2B 6NB
www.unicef.org.uk
Child Rights Information Network:
www.crin.org

Woodland Trust
Autumn Park, Dysart Road, Grantham
Lincs NG31 6LL

WWF – UK
Panda House, Weyside Park, Godalming
Surrey GU7 1XR
Tel: 01483 426 444
www.wwf-uk.org